EMPIRE'S
EDGE

EMPIRE'S

The Approach of Winter in the Arctic.

EDGE

American Society
in Nome, Alaska
1898–1934

PRESTON JONES

UNIVERSITY OF ALASKA PRESS

FAIRBANKS

For Annemarie, my Alaskan

© 2007 University of Alaska Press
P.O. Box 756240
Fairbanks, AK 99775-6240

Printed in the United States

Cover and interior design: Dixon J. Jones, Rasmuson Library Graphics
Cover image: "Guitar Player," Lomen Family Collection, acc. no. 72-71-1409, Archives, Alaska and Polar Regions Department, University of Alaska Fairbanks.
Back cover image: "Nome 1907," Lomen Family Collection, acc. no. 72-71-1697N, Archives, Alaska and Polar Regions Department, University of Alaska Fairbanks.
Title page illustration: "The Approach of Winter" on the Bering Sea. Lomen Family Collection, acc. no. 72-71-1036, Archives, Alaska and Polar Regions Department, University of Alaska Fairbanks.

Library of Congress Cataloging-in-Publication Data

Jones, Preston, 1966–
Empire's edge : American society in Nome, Alaska, 1898–1934 / by Preston Jones.
 p. cm.
Includes bibliographical references.
ISBN-13: 978-1-889963-89-1 (pbk. : alk. paper)
ISBN-10: 1-889963-89-5 (pbk. : alk. paper)
1. Nome (Alaska)—History. 2. Nome (Alaska)—Social life and customs. 3. Nome (Alaska)—Social conditions. 4. Group identity—Alaska—Nome—History—19th century. 5. Group identity—Alaska—Nome—History—20th century. 6. Community life—Alaska—Nome—History—19th century. 7. Community life—Alaska—Nome—History—20th century. 8. Frontier and pioneer life—Alaska—Nome. I. Title.
F914.N6J66 2007
979.8′6—dc22   2006010050

CONTENTS

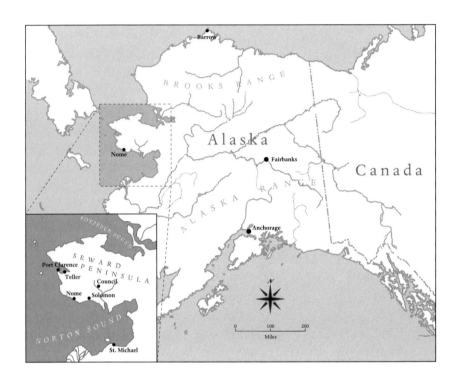

Map of Alaska *with inset showing the Seward Peninsula and location of Nome and nearby towns.*

PREFACE

In the 1915 edition of Nome High School's yearbook, the *Aurora*, Alfred J. Lomen wrote that "history is philosophy teaching by example."[1] Those words are apt, for as I began to research the story of Nome's first years, I wanted to know what its residents thought about America's expanding global influence. Nome came into being at the same time the United States was becoming an imperial power. I wondered how this context influenced the way Nomeites saw and spoke about themselves. I also wanted to know if Nome's residents tried to reproduce in the far north the culture they had known in what they would soon call the Outside. I was curious about how Nome's residents dealt with isolation. In short, to draw on young Lomen's words, I wanted to learn about the early Nomeites' philosophy of life and to study the American subculture they created so far from Alaska's capital, let alone any other center of power and influence. So this book is about perceptions—about the ways Nomeites perceived themselves, their city, and its place in the world. This book is also about Americans creating an easily identifiable American city in an environment unlike any other that had been settled by more than a few hundred Americans.

Alaskans who frequently read about Nome in their newspapers, and who share some of the hardships Nomeites face, are prone to forget the curiosity the city raises. "What do people do in Nome?" "Do they get along?" "How do they spend winters?" "How do they keep from going nuts?" These are among the predictable questions I have been asked when lecturing on early twentieth-century Nome in the Outside. And when I have shown Texans and Arkansans photographs of downtown Nome in 1905, they have been amazed to see that the pictures could have been taken in Illinois or Wisconsin or California. Audiences are surprised that early twentieth-century Nome looked so normal.

I admit that in the process of learning about the subculture the Nomeites created I became very impressed. I know it is not popular among academic historians to let one's admiration show but, while not indulging in mere celebration, I have made no effort to hide the esteem I feel for the achievements of Nome's early American inhabitants.

This book is rooted in primary sources and is the first scholarly book I am aware of that focuses on an Alaskan community. I wrote it with the literate general reader in mind, although I believe that professional historians will find it useful. The book owes a great deal to the work of Terrence Cole. His doctoral dissertation, "A History of the Nome Gold Rush: The Poor Man's Paradise" (1983), remains the best account of the events that made early twentieth-century Nome famous. Cole's Nome: "City of Golden Beaches" (1984) is a fine introduction to the history of Nome from the 1890s into the late twentieth century. Cole's objective was to provide an overview for a general audience, and the book, while not quite a town history, always keeps its focus on Nome.

This work is broader than Cole's work in that it seeks to place Nome within the context, first, of the Seward Peninsula, next of Alaska, and finally of North America. One of my goals is to show that while early twentieth-century Nome was unusual enough to merit a book-length study, it was also in many ways an ordinary American town. I do not focus on the flashy gold miners, husky con men, and dazzling bargirls of boomtown lore. Instead, I am concerned with ordinary people trying to make their way in an unusual environment.

Each of the chapters below brings the narrative closer to 1934, and the conclusion goes a little beyond that year, but this book does not follow a strict chronological scheme. And while the chapters are concerned with different themes, some topics reappear in consecutive chapters, for key ideas and ambitions born in Nome's first years evolved as time passed. Among these were the search for an industry that would make Nome a center of economic American influence, the desire for roads connecting Nome to other towns, and the impulse to advertise themselves to outsiders as Americans of a special kind.

A word about sources. I have relied on newspapers more than I would like. In a way, this has been unavoidable. Newspapers are to a town or city what a diary is to an individual. But newspapers are hardly disinterested and historians must use them judiciously. I take newspaper accounts at face value when there is good reason to do so, such as when a noncontroversial event is recorded without editorial commentary. It is true that by recording some things and leaving other things unrecorded, editors make history of their biases. But in a small city like Nome, where newspapers depended on subscribers and local businesses, genuinely important events could not go unmentioned. For this same reason, editorial commentary can be taken as representing at least a substantial portion of the population's opinion. Still, when editors' opinions are being cited, I make that clear. I assume that editors are speaking for some Nomeites; it is not possible that they spoke for all Nomeites at all times. A more particular reason I have had to rely fairly heavily on newspapers is that so much documentation that might otherwise have been useful—photographs, as well as court, municipal, and business records—was destroyed in Nome's great fire of 1934. Still, as I hope the bibliography shows, a substantial number of primary sources are available, and I have found that they usually corroborate what is found in Nome's newspapers.

For the genesis of this study, I wish to thank my parents, Mary and Ralph, who brought me up in a peripheral neighborhood of a peripheral city and thus laid the foundation for my interest in out-of-the-way places. My parents-in-law, Maria and Gerry of Eagle River, Alaska, put my family up for two research stints in the summers of 2003 and 2004. I must also mention Jitters, a café in Eagle River, whose staff put up with me as I sat for hours nursing cups of coffee, reading, and writing. Thanks to Cal Piston and the Faculty Development Committee at John Brown University for awarding me a Shipps Scholars Grant that paid for much of the research and writing costs; and to Simone Schroder, the indispensable interlibrary loan librarian at JBU.

Thanks to Stephen Haycox, of the University of Alaska Anchorage, and James Ducker, editor of *Alaska History*, for being very critical of my first forays into the history of Alaska. They forced me to become more serious. Portions of chapters 1 and 2 appear in an article of mine in *Alaska History* 19, no. 1–2 (Spring/Fall 2004), 25–43. The section on Natives in the introduction draws heavily on another paper of mine published in *Alaska History* 20, no. 2 (Fall 2005), 43–58. Thanks as well to Dan Sparkman, who invited me to lecture on Nome in his classroom at the Eagle River branch of the University of Alaska. Preparation for that lecture provided me with an opportunity to conceptualize the book's introduction.

Bruce Parham of the National Archives and Records Administration, Pacific Alaska Region, directed me to many excellent primary sources. He also provided me with some two hundred pages of primary documents he photocopied for personal use at the National Archives in Maryland. Diana Kodiak, also at NARA in Anchorage, was helpful, as were the staff at the municipal libraries in Eagle River and Anchorage—most especially Bruce Merrill. The same is true of Jude Baldwin of the Anchorage Museum of History and Art's library and the staff at University of Alaska Anchorage. Arlene Schmuland at UAA's archives and manuscripts department pointed me to a few excellent resources.

Rose Speranza and Caroline Atuk, of the University of Alaska Fairbanks, are serious archivists and were very helpful to me in the course of a brief and intense period of research. Bev Gelzer, of the Carrie McLain Memorial Museum in Nome, provided me with a great deal of information as did the museum's director, Laura Samuelson, whose enthusiasm for Nome and its history is infectious. Laura provided useful criticism on an early draft of this book.

Dr. Erica Hill was my first contact at the University of Alaska Press and she is a professional, perspicacious, and patient editor. Her comments on early drafts of this book were uniformly helpful. I also thank the anonymous reviewers of this manuscript whose comments and criticisms helped to make this book better than it would have been otherwise.

The work of my student, Kyle Raymond, on Nome–Siberia and U.S.–Russia relations in the early twentieth century was thorough and useful. I am glad to be able to thank this historian in the making for his help.

This book is dedicated to my wife and best friend, Annemarie. *Dyna pam y bydd dyn yn gadael ei dad a'i fam ac yn glynu wrth ei wraig.*

Any errors in fact or judgment that survive in this book are my responsibility. I welcome communications at *pjones@jbu.edu.*

Preston Jones
Siloam Springs, Arkansas

INTRODUCTION

CONTEXT AND THEMES

There is much more to the small city of Nome than lives in collective memory. Yes, the well-documented and iconic gold miners, bargirls, gunslingers, and con artists are all part of Nome's early history.[1] But that city, built on the southwestern coast of Alaska's Seward Peninsula, moved beyond these symbols within a couple years of its founding. Early Nomeites, nearly 80 percent of whom were miners and whose average age in 1900 was thirty-five, did not romanticize the gold rush when it was in progress, and some continued to refuse to do so in later years.[2] In the crude but provocative words of one of Nome's public school officials and famous dogsled drivers, A. A. "Scotty" Allan, gold

> throws off rays that devour the soul and corrode society. Gold, like passion, makes glands work until the human mind goes berserk. Naked gold, like the nude feminine form, may be divinely lovely or devilishly provocative to lust, greed, hate, crime. I learned this first-hand in the Klondike rush, later in Nome, and all through the Alaska gold fields.[3]

The gist of Allan's observation was that a man's lust for gold, like his carnal desire, needs to be tamed, channeled, civilized. If that lust had not been subdued in Nome, the city probably would not have survived.

In the process of wrenching order out of chaos, Nomeites did something extraordinary: they built an easily recognizable American community in a most uncommon environment. As a writer for *Harper's Weekly* put it, "in the face of nature's most severe obstacles," Nome's settlers had created "one of the present wonders of Uncle Sam's domains."[4] So while there is much that is unique about

Nome, the most striking thing about the city is its normality—or "normalcy," as Americans began to say in the 1920s. The city's mundane Americanness always struck, and usually surprised, visitors.

In this book, I link the admittedly infelicitous term "Americanness" to my main theme, namely, that the Americans who went to Nome forged a permanent, recognizably American subculture—Americanness—in an entirely novel environment.[5] It would be difficult—probably impossible—to define early twentieth-century "Americanness." For every characteristic one could point to as representatively American, there are exceptions. Between 1898 and 1934, for example, capitalism was American, but so was socialism. Resistance to governmental regulation was American, but so was its acceptance. Litigious courtroom warfare was American, but so was neighborliness. Making an easy definition of Americanness even more difficult was the mass immigration to the U.S. that took place around 1900, when Americanness encompassed the "Little Italys" and "Little Polands" of New York and Chicago.

All of these phenomena existed in Nome. Nearly 35 percent of the first Nomeites were foreign-born, although by 1900 three-quarters of these immigrants were naturalized American citizens. But just as complexity did not create impenetrable ambiguity in cities in the Lower 48, the so-called "Outside"—no one doubted that Unitarian Boston and rural Baptist Georgia were equally, although quite differently, American—so Nome's Americanness was as obvious as the oddness of its treeless environment. Physically, and perhaps psychologically, Nome was set apart. But visitors among Nomeites, and Nomeites among Outsiders, did not feel foreign to one another. And given the incessant challenges and disappointments they faced, the Nomeites' success was a remarkable achievement. There are few cities that merit scholarly books about them simply because they exist. Nome does deserve such a book.

In these pages I report on aspects of Nome's existence from its beginnings at the end of the nineteenth century to 1934, the year of a devastating fire. My approach is more descriptive than analytical, and I offer readers a more complete picture of an early twentieth-century Alaskan city than has been available until now. I relate some of the ways Nomeites created a city that looked and felt American, not only to residents but to visitors (chapter 1); I describe how Nomeites saw their city within the context of America's rapidly growing empire at the beginning of the twentieth century (chapter 2); I chronicle Nome's victory in a contest for survival with other settlements on the Seward Peninsula (chapter 3). I also report on Nome's public life—sports, civic culture, education, and politics (chapter 4), and recount some of the effects of the First World War on the city (chapter 5). Finally, I describe the atmosphere on the eve of, and some of the responses to, the disastrous fire of 1934 (chapter 6). Along the way, we find Nomeites raising American flags, dancing, writing essays, keeping diaries, arguing about politics, suing one another, marrying, divorcing, getting sick, trading in Siberia, and preparing for military invasions from Japan and the Soviet Union.

From time to time I place events in Nome within a broader American context. I do so because one can learn a lot about trends in the U.S. by observing them in the microcosm of Nome. In the first two chapters, I also include commentary on events in Canada so as to situate some trends in Nome within a broader North American context.

The hopes Nomeites had for their city in the first few decades of the twentieth century were often dashed. But while there is sometimes a whiff of the ridiculous hanging about the schemes Nomeites promoted until 1934, there was never a lack of tenacity driving the schemers. And enough of their plans would work—enough would pan out (so to speak)—to keep the city going. The American flag kept flying in a place hundreds of miles closer to Russia than it is to any other American settlement of more than a few hundred souls. So one theme of this book is tenacity—the tenacity of merchants and dreamers, of capitalists and socialists, of teenagers submitting to drills in Latin grammar one hundred miles south of the Arctic Circle.

Making success possible in the first place required commitment from public-minded people whose enlightened self-interest benefited their city. More than any other family, the Lomens, who appear often in this book, were a stabilizing force in Nome and the western Seward Peninsula. In Nome's early years, Gudbrand Lomen, the patriarch, was a prominent city lawyer. Later he became a federal judge, then Nome's mayor, and eventually the U.S. district attorney with an office in the city. His son, George, was a municipal judge and city assessor. The brothers Ralph, Alfred, and Carl ran a pharmacy, a clothing store, and a photographic studio,[6] and they outfitted ships for Canadians who wanted to claim Wrangel Island for the British Empire.[7] When a reindeer herd on Baffin Island needed an expert to save it, the job was offered to Carl (he declined). When in 1927 a schemer in Malaya envisioned a railroad connecting Chicago to Peking via Nome, he unsuccessfully sought Carl as an ally.[8] When a search was organized for a lost pilot, Ralph was put in charge. When important people visited town, they dined with the Lomens.[9] Lomen and Company, which raised

reindeer for food and clothing until it was closed by the federal government in
the late 1930s, was established in 1913. Helen Lomen, like her brothers, showed
her smarts at school and later published a children's novel about Native life
in Alaska, *Taktuk: An Arctic Boy* (1928). "We all took part in civic affairs," Carl
wrote in his memoirs, "and interested ourselves in community matters that we
believed would prove beneficial to Nome and to Alaska as a whole."[10]

WOMEN

While most of the sources cited in this study were written by men—in this, too,
Nome was ordinary—it is important to remember that, after the frequently cha-
otic first two years, Nome's stability was the work of both sexes. The words of
one male observer are patronizing but complimentary. There were a thousand
women in the Nome region, he wrote in 1900,

> and they have, as usual, taken vigorous action with the sanitary question;
> brave, noble, energetic, self-sacrificing American women—God bless them!—
> mothers, wives, daughters, sisters, and sweethearts who will urge upon those
> near and dear to them the pressing need of better sanitation.[11]

The influence of women in early Nome society was everywhere: women's
social clubs provided entertainment, public order, and lodging (see chapter 1). In
short order, Nome's female students began to write essays and poems on life in
the city (see chapter 4). And Nome's young women went to college at a higher
rate than their counterparts Outside. In 1910 about 40 percent of American
college students were women; around the same time, 70 percent of the college
students who had graduated from Nome's high school were women.[12] And
while primary sources written by women comprise a minority of the whole,
this study would be diminished without the photographs of Elizabeth Wood,
the papers of Ruthmary McDowell, and the books and articles by Elizabeth
Robins, Esther Birdsall Darling, Mary Lee Davis, Alice Palmer Henderson, and
Ella Higginson, among others.

There was little social conflict of any kind in Nome up to 1934. One of the
themes of this book is that life in Nome was enough of a challenge; there was
meager time or energy to spend on strained social relations—including relations between the sexes. As was the case Outside, Nome's Women's Christian
Temperance Union dogged the city's booze peddlers, but they spoke for the
majority, which voted for the "Alaska Bone-Dry Law" of 1918 (see chapter 4).

FIGURE 1. *Eighteen-year-old Lottie Renny and an unnamed Australian on the Bering Sea ice, Nome, c. 1903–1909. Photographer Arthur L. Bell. Carrie M. McLain Memorial Museum (Nome), Arthur L. Bell Photograph Collection, no. N-159.*

NATIVES

If sources written by women are few, documentary sources from Natives in the period under study are even rarer.[13] To my knowledge, not one of the texts listed in the bibliography was penned by a Native. What this points to is a simple reality: Literacy is something Westerners valued, promoted, and took for granted as a rudiment of civilization. In the same way that gold came to mean something to the Seward Peninsula's Natives only after Westerners gave it meaning, so literacy became useful to the Nome region's Natives only after the Nome region (as we think of it) came into existence—that is, after Westerners labeled it, settled it, exploited it, and began to write about it. The influence of Yankees on Natives would be deep and unalterable, and some Nomeites and those who wrote about them used the customarily condescending language of the day, referring to Natives as, for example, "Uncle Sam's adopted children" and "primitive yet promising peoples."[14] But Natives in turn influenced how Nomeites dressed, talked, studied, traveled, decorated their homes, engaged in commerce, and presented themselves to the outside world.

While unpleasant newspaper commentary on Natives—"they are a nuisance to the community"[15]—reflects abstract ideas and general negative opinions some Nomeites held, they do not tell us about how Nomeites behaved day to day. At the level of abstraction, Natives were "slant-eyed" people who spoke "gibberish."[16] In Nome's earliest years, especially, non-Native anxieties may have been projected onto Natives, thus helping to create anti-Native feeling.[17] This might account for the sometimes nasty tone of the *Nome Nugget*, which one historian has documented.[18] But once Nome achieved stability, there was less non-Native angst to foist onto Natives and, before long, Natives became Nomeites' assistants, workmates, fellow traders, fellow Christians, and customers. In 1917 the *Nugget* announced, without comment or any hint of disapproval, that all Nomeites were invited to the Easter service at the Eskimo Methodist church.[19] (Nomeites felt free to attend Native worship services for years before the 1917 invitation.[20]) In the same year the *Nome Industrial Worker* reported—curtly and without commentary of the well-what-can-you-expect-from-those-people? variety—that two Natives had been arraigned for rape.[21] And all the while Nomeites relied on Natives to help them with adventures far from the comforts of Nome.[22] Ada Blackjack, the best known of the Seward Peninsula's Natives in Nome's first decades, was a "city Eskimo" who brushed her teeth, sewed clothing for miners, and learned to read the Bible and honor the American flag. But as the sole survivor of an expedition to Wrangel Island in the early 1920s she became a role model, a teacher to her teachers: she was heroic, an exemplary Christian, "the first Eskimo heroine in history."[23]

Early twentieth-century Nome was typically American in that it was a segregated society. Not long after the *Nome Nugget* complained about Natives "hanging about the stores and saloons, learning plenty of vice and little good," a twenty-acre voluntary reservation of sorts was established at the mouth of Quartz Creek, twenty miles west of Nome. In 1906 a similar operation was initiated seven miles farther west.[24] Many of the Natives who still came into town did so only in the summer months, to fish and to sell handcrafts, although some sold crab there in the winter.[25] The striking thing is that, while Nome was segregationist (though never completely and not very successfully), it was not hostile to Natives.[26] We know that Natives were regularly in town: the Catholic Church in Nome built a heated trading room for Natives to use,[27] and visitors to Nome observed and wrote about the Natives in the city.[28] Natives patronized Nome's stores such as the Lomen brothers' pharmacy without difficulty, and the Lomens displayed Native art in the store's windows, to the applause of the *Industrial Worker*.[29] Appreciation for Native art was something that Nome's rock-ribbed Republicans, like the Lomens, and socialist scribblers, like the editors at the *Industrial Worker*, had in common.

There were other ways that Native influence worked its way into the lives and thoughts of Nome's Yankees. Multiple photographs reveal that soon after the city was founded, some Nomeites began to dress like Natives, especially in the winter.[30] Photographs of Nomeites in groups—which show some of them dressed in Western clothing and others wearing Native clothing—are easy to find.[31] This is important because, save for those who went into their first Nome winter unprepared and, therefore, had no choice, Nomeites did not have to adopt Native dress—and they did not do so for lack of options, as a perusal of newspaper advertisements from Nome's clothing merchants makes clear.[32] Nome's non-Natives could easily have dressed through the winter like urban Canadians or Minnesotans, who also endured uncomfortable cold, and much of the time they did dress that way. But the fact that they sometimes dressed like Alaska Natives suggests a couple things. First, it indicates that the personal walls of separation that existed between Nomeites and Natives contained substantial gaps. Obviously, to wear Native clothing was to make oneself look like a Native, as the editors of Mary Lee Davis's *Uncle Sam's Attic* felt obliged to acknowledge in conjunction with a photo of the author dressed in a parka.[33] This, in turn, suggests that looking something like a Native could not have been all that bad. Thus the clichéd, early twentieth-century rhetoric of unequivocal Anglo-Saxon superiority is thrown into doubt, for it is difficult to see why people would choose to dress like people they looked down on, or loathed, or merely pitied. A better explanation is that Nomeites sometimes chose to dress like Natives because they liked Native clothing, they recognized its usefulness and attractiveness, and they appreciated the skill of the Natives who had made it.

Native clothing also helped to shape how Nomeites presented themselves to the world beyond Alaska. Consider that pictures of Nomeites dressed like Natives were used to advertise and promote the All-Alaska Sweepstakes dogsled races. Save for their European facial features, the Nomeites pictured were not distinguishable from Natives in their own winter clothing.[34] Or consider that when, during the Alaska–Yukon Pacific Exposition, a pamphlet was printed to inform readers that Nome's basketball team was playing exhibition games

FIGURE 2. *"Eskimos at bookstore," Elizabeth Wood Collection, acc. no. 2000-101-402, Archives, Alaska and Polar Regions Department, University of Alaska Fairbanks.*

throughout the country, its cover depicted the team dressed in Native clothing. The basketball team's tour would "show to the people of the United States the kind of American citizens that are developing this frozen empire," the pamphlet read. "These young men are samples of the intrepid and indomitable explorers of the Northland."[35] Their fortitude was not symbolized by images of American industrial or military might, or even by drawings of rugged gold miners, which would have worked just as well as a marketing gimmick. They were symbolized, rather, by what everyone would have immediately recognized as Native dress.

It may be that this was a way for Nomeites to present themselves as exotic, but that does not amount to a complete explanation, for Nomeites also dressed like Natives when no one else was looking. The representation of Nomeites to outsiders as Americans dressed like Natives was accurate; that this might have helped with marketing Nome to non-Alaskans is incidental. Nomeites presented themselves as Americans of a different kind, and the differences were symbolized by Native clothing.

FIGURE 3. *"Saxophone band," Lomen Family Collection, acc. no. 72-71-1341, Archives, Alaska and Polar Regions Department, University of Alaska Fairbanks.*

The more one pays attention to the primary sources, the more ubiquitous the quiet influence of Natives on Nome's residents appears. James Wickersham, the federal judge and future Congressional delegate for Alaska, studied Native culture, decorated his room in the Golden Gate Hotel with Native art, and presented a learned paper on Natives to the Nome Literary Society.[36] This points to the general interest in Natives among educated Nomeites. Elsewhere in town, in some of Nome's most genteel homes, photographs of Natives graced the walls.[37]

Native girls were sometimes compared positively to Nome's bargirls, and news of marriages—even of references to physical intimacy—between Native women and non-Native men appeared very early in the *Nome Gold Digger*.[38] A poignant example of mutual influence comes to us from Charles Madsen. The Native girl he wanted to marry had converted to Catholicism under the tutelage of a missionary from Quebec, so for her sake he gave up Protestantism.[39]

Natives were seen, at least by some, as morally superior to non-Natives. As early as February of 1900 the *Gold Digger* observed that American alcohol, greed, and immorality corrupted Natives.[40] Six years later the *Daily Gold Digger* pitied the "poor Eskimo!" who was learning the "white man's" ways.[41] Finally, in her very public essay—an essay that certainly could have been censored by school authorities—the graduating senior Helen Kreps wrote that

> [b]efore the coming of the white men to Alaska the Eskimo were a simple,
> honest, affectionate people. Stealing was so entirely unknown to them that
> after the arrival of the white strangers they were very much surprised to find
> that their boats and nets which they had left on the shore had disappeared.[42]

Surely "noble savage" mythology is at work in these lines, but they also suggest something that is as fascinating as it is surprising—namely, that people who had grown up in the highly moral public environment of Victorian America were willing to concede that, in some ways, the Seward Peninsula's Natives were their betters.

Like the United States generally, early twentieth-century Nome was both a segregated society and a melting pot. Nomeites did not protest against segregationist schemes, but they studied Native culture, they wore Native clothing, they profited from Native innovations, and a few of them married Native women.

The following quotation sheds light on the meeting of cultures in early twentieth-century Nome. "Come and dine with me at the Royal Cafe," writes T. A. Rickard,

The place is crowded but clean; the well intended efforts of a piano and a violin give a touch of gaiety, and the crowd that passes along the main street can be watched with interest while the reindeer stew or the roast ptarmigan is being prepared. The Eskimo give color to the scene; the women in their pink and yellow parkas and wolverine hoods look like ladies on their way to a party; the men in fur ruffles and light drill parkas wear visored caps or else go bare-headed with masses of long black hair trimmed with a Dutch cut. Two Eskimo carry the skin of the polar bear on a long pole. Others have carved whalebone for sale. Dogs are numerous. The bright tints of the native costume produce a chromatic liveliness unusual in a mining camp. The huskies and the malamutes accompany the Eskimo and suggest arctic life. An occasional Saxon of fresh complexion looks very pink amid these black and oily denizens of the North.[43]

The Native presence in the Nome diner is at first both alluring and exotic, and it points to the mingling of Nome's Natives and non-Natives.

Still, it remains true that, for the majority of Nomeites, Natives were mostly irrelevant or ornamental; they did not play a significant role in the emerging objectives Euro-Americans had for Nome. In this book, I concentrate on those objectives, describing how Euro-Americans strove to make Nome an American city. To be sure, their vision of "American" was subjective and failed to incorporate Native people in meaningful ways either socially or politically. However, this vision was also the prime mover in the development of Nome in the late nineteenth and early twentieth centuries.

GOLD

The Nome gold rush reached its most fevered stage in the summer of 1900 and marked the end of a series of major nineteenth-century gold discoveries around the world—in Australia, South Africa, the Canadian Yukon, and elsewhere in Alaska. The continental United States also experienced numerous strikes in the nineteenth century—in Georgia, Colorado, Montana, and, of course, California.[44]

The Nome rush helped to put an end to arguments in favor of the U.S. instituting a silver-based currency alongside the gold standard. This had been the central political issue of the presidential election of 1896. Democratic candidate William Jennings Bryan famously decried the malefactors of wealth who would crucify mankind on an expensive cross of gold. But the gold sent to the Outside from Nome, like the takings from the Klondike before it, made currency easier for workers and farmers to acquire. The year before gold was first discovered by Euro-Americans in the Nome region, *The Nation* opined that the gold rushes of the late nineteenth century suggested that even the deity was on the side of the "gold-bugs."[45] The Nome rush seemed to prove the point.

Every major nineteenth-century gold rush took place under either the British Union Jack or the Stars and Stripes. Beginning with the events in California in 1848, this was taken as proof that Providence favored the Anglo-Saxons or, as they would later be generically called, the English-speaking peoples. Both Spain and Mexico had possessed California, but those countries did not plumb the depths of its mineral wealth. The United States, on the other hand, had hardly taken possession of California when gold seemed to spring from the ground.

Such was the trend. Russia had owned Alaska and Dutch-speaking Afrikaaners were a large presence in South Africa, but neither gained as much from the gold in those territories as did the English speakers, along with the non-English speakers who were willing to settle under Anglo-Saxon flags. The sense of privilege that came with being so favored by Providence was nourished by, and spurred, British and American imperialism.

EMPIRE

The rush to Nome took place at the same time that the U.S. was becoming an imperial power. As a result of its war against Spain in 1898, the U.S. acquired Puerto Rico, Guam, and the Philippines. In the same year, although for reasons not directly linked to the war, the U.S. annexed Hawai'i. In 1900, moreover, American troops joined with those of Britain, France, and Japan to put down a Chinese uprising against foreigners. Now China would trade with the industrializing world whether its patriots liked it or not. In other words, as had been true since the early 1600s, American influence and power were marching westward—this time into the western Pacific. Much of the country's economic and military strategic focus was on the Pacific Ocean. As the *Alaska–Yukon Magazine* put it, the Pacific, formerly the world's backyard, had become the world's field of competition.[46]

Given Nome's place on the Pacific Rim, it is understandable that the men and women who chose to move there in the first years of the twentieth century believed that they were on the cutting edge of American empire and international influence. They gained indirect support for this belief from men and women of consequence. In *Alaska: An Empire in the Making*, a thick book published in 1912 and dedicated to the National Press Club, John Jasper Underwood observed that Alaska's coal was fifteen hundred miles closer to the Philippines than it was the coal base at San Francisco, on which the U.S. fleet relied. The implication was that the base at San Francisco should be replaced by, or at least complemented with, a base in Alaska.[47]

Also lurking in the background when Nome was developing and stabilizing was Japan's rise to world power status. Japan joined the European countries in exploiting China; and like Germany, Britain, France, Portugal, the Netherlands, and Russia, along with the United States, Japan had designs on Asian territory. The resulting competition for colonies partly explains why the U.S. decided to stay in the Philippine islands after liberating them from Spain. The U.S. also knew that other powers coveted Hawai'i. By the early 1900s, it seemed that all lands washed by Pacific waters were, or seemed to be, related in some way to European, American, or Japanese imperial ventures. The establishment of an American outpost in Nome was no different.

At the same time, some observers looked to Siberia as the "land of the future." In Siberia, some thought, the Russians would create a bulwark for European

FIGURE 4. *Alaska–Yukon–Pacific Exposition emblem. University of Washington Libraries, Special Collections, neg. no. Nowell x236.*

civilization.[48] The shores of eastern Siberia were hundreds of miles nearer to Nome than the quaint streets of Juneau or Skagway; they were much closer than the great ports of Seattle or San Francisco. If Siberia were a land of promise, Nomeites would be there to capitalize on it, and they expected to do so.

Given their place on the Pacific coast and their proximity to a region across the Bering Strait that promised wealth, Nomeites can be forgiven for indulging in the inflated imperial rhetoric that fills the pages of chapter 2. In the late nineteenth and early twentieth centuries, such rhetoric was, after all, ubiquitous in the public discourse of industrialized nations. It was also Alaska-wide, and Alaska's boosters knew it appealed to Americans generally. The official seal of the Alaska–Yukon–Pacific Exposition in Seattle (1909), for example, depicted three graceful ladies (Figure 4). One is a Japanese woman holding a model ship. Another is a Caucasian holding a model train. The third, symbolizing Alaska, is situated between these two—she presides over them, really—and she clenches gold nuggets larger than her hands. The Japanese and American women are dressed darkly; Alaska is white. Japan and America seem troubled; Alaska is serenely prominent.[49]

This representation of Alaska was certainly driven by more benign motives than those of the fraudulent Reynolds–Alaska Development Company. ("The only problem facing [the company's] gold mines," Morgan Sherwood observes, "was the absence of gold.")[50] But Henry Derr Reynolds's effort to raise money for a bogus enterprise via the promotion of Alaska as the "keystone of American supremacy on the Pacific Ocean" illustrates the fact that, by 1904, Americans saw Alaska through imperial lenses.

Related to this outlook was the belief, or the claim, that Alaska's early twentieth-century pioneers were akin to the settlers of Jamestown and Plymouth Rock—that their work built upon foundations laid by John Smith, William Bradford, John Winthrop, Roger Williams, and Anne Hutchinson. Nome's early settlers, resembling the *Mayflower*'s company, "were the last of their kind we shall witness on this continent." In establishing a government for themselves, Nome's first settlers were like the "Pilgrim fathers that landed on Plymouth Rock."[51] This theme was promoted by no less a figure than President Warren Harding.[52]

SOCIAL DARWINISM

The evocation of the Pilgrims' and early Virginians' spirits stirred memories of success in the face of sometimes excruciating hardship. For many in the early twentieth century, that hardship would seem the stuff of Darwinian struggle, and success despite hardship was considered an emblem of superior strength, intelligence, and hardiness. Survivors endured and conquered because they were more fit than the competition.

According to the outlook of the day, usually referred to as "social Darwinism," what was true of individuals was also true of nations: the strongest, cleverest, and fittest nations would win the global sweepstakes for colonies, wealth, power, and prestige. As Charles Darwin himself put it in 1871, "a nation which produced... the greatest number of highly intellectual, energetic, brave, patriotic, and benevolent men, would generally prevail over less favored nations."[53] Thus, like Hawai'i and the captured possessions of the moribund Spanish empire, Alaska presented Americans with an opportunity to hone their strength and cleverness. John Underwood praised Alaska's rivers because they had the "strength of Titans" and, he suggested, Alaska was the perfect match for a young and vigorous nation, for "in all her moods she engenders strength and virility."[54]

This kind of language pervades writing about early American Alaska in general and Nome in particular. Alaska's residents, the memoirist J. A. Hellenthal tells us, were recruited "largely from among the most adventurous, most daring, and most capable of all other lands."[55] Another writer carried this banner even unto the chambers of Nome's prostitutes who, somehow, always brimmed with wit, wisdom, and more than the standard helping of vigor.

> Nome's percentage of girls and prostitutes... were of an unusually high type, and for a very good reason. It took not only courage but health and physical strength for women to stand the northern winter under frontier conditions. Most of the prostitutes were big, husky girls, girls with a good deal of pride and spirit.[56]

Or, as Judge James Wickersham wrote years after leaving Nome, the city's "sporting women were... of a more robust class."[57]

GOVERNMENT

Alaska historian Stephen Haycox writes that Alaska's gold rush spurred the federal government to pay attention to the territory and to organize it.[58] Many of Nome's early settlers would have agreed that the government had played an important role in organizing Alaska, but few would say that the government did

enough to attract more settlers to Alaska or to make the district more livable
for the people who did settle there.

In the early twentieth century, Alaskans liked to notice that the federal government extracted far more wealth from the territory than it returned in the
form of roads and other services. In this respect, Alaska resembled an Old World
colony, and Alaskans had read about what earlier colonists with names like
Patrick Henry and Samuel Adams had done when they felt oppressed by a distant government. A few Alaskans, like the earlier revolutionaries, would call
for separation from the mother country and, ironically, for Alaska's annexation
to British Canada.[59] But among the large majority in Nome and other Alaskan
settlements not attracted to sedition, there still grew up a tenacious myth of
government neglect.

A paradox is that this myth was boosted in the early years by Sam C. Dunham,
who drew income as an agent of the federal government, first as a statistician
for the Department of Labor (1897–1898) and then as an agent of the Twelfth
Census (1899–1900). Numerous newspapers in Alaska published his poem
"Alaska to Uncle Sam," where we find the district

> Sitting on my greatest glacier,
> With my feet in Bering Sea,
> I am thinking, cold and lonely,
> Of the way [Uncle Sam's] treated me.[60]

Elsewhere Dunham depicts Alaska as a "proud-souled woman" praying for
"the dawn of civil rights" and as a treasure house left in the lurch. He ends
his collection of verse with the suggestion that the American press, following the government's lead, was less interested in Alaska than in China, the
Philippines, and the Boer War. On this point, Dunham was right. However
great the mineral yield in Alaska in 1899 and 1900, the Spanish-American War,
China's Boxer Rebellion, and Britain's war against the Afrikaaners in South
Africa seemed to be of greater long-term international significance. Alaska's
newspapers dwelt on those topics too, although, to be sure, not at the expense
of local matters.

In an obvious way, though, Dunham was quite wrong. Most of the poems
he collected into his book of 1901 had, after all, been published earlier in prominent newspapers such as the *New York Sun*, *Washington Post*, and *San Francisco
Examiner*;[61] and the countless international newspaper articles and pamphlets

about the Klondike and Nome strikes that absorbed so much public attention hardly suggest indifference to Alaska.[62] One senses that Dunham's wailing was, in part, a *schtick*—Alaska provided him with material that gained him entry into the offices of editors and publications of national promise. But many in Nome took his disgruntled musings as gospel.

Nomeites did have reason for dissatisfaction. In 1900 some of them lost a great deal of money to the machinations of a corrupt federal judge in Nome, Arthur Noyes, and a Republican Party influence peddler, Alexander McKenzie. Indeed, even in an age famous for corrupt officials, Nome seemed to have more than its share. In addition to Noyes and McKenzie, the postmaster, Joseph Wright, was removed from office for incompetence, while a derelict U.S. attorney and jury-tampering U.S. Marshall came under fire.[63]

There is also the fact that the territorial legislature, which began work in 1913, was not empowered by the federal government to accomplish a great deal. It did pass legislation providing for the compulsory education of non-Native students and it sought to ensure that Alaska's doctors and dentists were qualified. But it had to ask Congress to pass legislation to award Alaskans, fearful of their caribou herds' decimation by wolves, $10 for every wolf killed.[64] This struck close to home. On a typical day, the welfare of animals that settlers relied on seemed more pressing than the competence of dentists, but legal remedy was thousands of miles away. Here, in part, is where a belief in the story of government neglect gained support.[65]

The other side of the ledger is, however, also weighty. In Nome's first years, agents in the employ of the federal government improved health standards by establishing a quarantine center outside of town, promoting vaccinations, and by piping in clean water from outlying areas.[66] Summertime Nome in 1900 may have been near anarchy, but it never plunged into chaos, thanks largely to federal troops sent to the city, first from St. Michael, and soon after from Fort Davis, established a few miles east of the city. These soldiers guarded mines while their ownership was being determined and, after storms, they watched over Front Street's ruins to prevent looting. The soldiers helped to establish and maintain communication systems; they helped to link Nome and St. Michael via undersea cable.[67] Fort Davis was also a center of Nome's social life.[68] And when, in the fall of 1900, Nome appeared to be heading into a potentially crime-drenched winter, the U.S. Revenue Cutter Service illegally but usefully rounded up suspected thugs and hauled them away.

Some federal officials in Nome had been corrupt, but other honest federal officials put them out of business.[69] Rex Beach's novel about corruption in Nome, *The Spoilers* (1906), sold well for many years precisely because Nome had become a stable city that was safe for families and merchants. Now the city's early crime could be romanticized.

Then there was the problem of mail. Early Nomeites fretted about few things more than mail—or, more precisely, the lack of efficient mail delivery. Certainly no one liked to wait weeks or months to get letters from home, friends, or business associates. The government found itself on the receiving end of this anxiety. But, given the circumstances, the government served Nome and its inhabitants well. A letter sent first class from Nome cost the patron two cents, but it actually cost hundreds of times that to deliver a letter to the Outside. One mail shipment from Kotzebue to Nome cost about $259; a shipment from Nome to Unalakleet cost about $263. Add to these costs the distance a piece of mail would have to travel before reaching its destination in the American Midwest or east, and one can see that it was expensive for the government to supply even the lackluster service it did.[70] Yet Nomeites never had to pay mail rates higher than those paid in Michigan or Alabama, Maine or Arkansas.

This is not to say that there were no grounds for the complaints Nomeites made against the federal government. But recognition among Nome's residents of what actually had been done by the federal government was rarely as strong as the vision of what it might have done, and the vision of outsiders was sometimes better than the Nomeites'. In 1900, one writer in the Outside noted that he had received a letter from Nome that had taken only two months and twenty-four days to arrive. Considering that the letter had traversed a few thousand miles of land until recently considered uninhabitable, George Edward Adams wrote, the feat seemed almost miraculous.[71]

TRANSIENCE

In addition to concerns over empire and the role of government in settling and promoting Nome, the city's public life was characterized by transience. Throughout Nome's first decades, miners, travelers, military personnel, and others came and went; many of Nome's summer workers lived in the Outside the rest of the year; and traders dropped off and picked up goods, meeting with friends in Nome as they passed through.[72] Even Nome's early newspapermen—energetic town boosters—hardly modeled hanging in for the long haul.

Harry Steel, editor and publisher of the *Nome News*, and J. F. A. Strong of the *Nome Nugget*, were gone by the end of 1906.[73] Judge James Wickersham, who did so much to help early Nomeites see that the law would prevail on the tundra, and who had pressing official responsibilities elsewhere, stayed in town less than a year. After 1907, the mark of a relatively successful mining company in Nome was only to survive for several years.[74] Certainly the high cost of living and doing business in Nome contributed to population instability. Sometimes mining operations found that hauling equipment through the Seward Peninsula was too costly to be worth the effort. Better to wash one's hands and walk away.[75] It is not surprising, therefore, that at the end of the 1920s one businessman thought that Nome was dying. Soon, he wrote, "there will be only the memory left."[76] Nome had its own community stalwarts such as the Lomen family, although as the years went by even they spent greater amounts of time Outside. Carl Lomen was away from Nome through much of the 1920s and early 1930s.[77]

This high degree of transience was partly the result of the city having been founded by people who, before going there, had experienced movement from place to place. A preponderance of Nome's first settlers were from western states (especially California), which in 1900 were still being settled, and around 70 percent of the first Nomeites had gone to the city from a state or nation different from those in which they had been born.[78]

One result of the constant movement in, through, and out of town was a sense that Nomeites were at the mercy of outsiders—especially outsiders from Seattle. "In the beginning," one Alaskan newspaper observed, "Seattle created Alaska and its commerce."[79] There was much to support this view. Everyone knew that Seattle's economic growth had been spurred by Alaska's gold rushes;[80] and in 1922 some ninety men were employed constructing a dredge for Hammon Consolidated Gold Fields, two-thirds of whom came from the Outside.[81] Alaska's economic reliance on decisions made in Seattle remains a source of concern in the early twenty-first century.

Community-building tenacity alongside transience; Nome's existence on the American periphery combined with hopes that the city would play an important role in the expansion of American power; a strong sense of independence matching the need for government assistance; ordinary, if multifaceted, Americanness planted in an extraordinary natural environment; Natives both quasi-segregated and relied on—such are the choppy waters Nome's men and women navigated up to 1934. Such are the paradoxes that make up the story of Nome related in the pages that follow.

I DO NOT LOOK WITH DESPONDING EYES *into the future. The nations every-where,—in Europe and Asia,—the new and the old, are moving onward and upward as never before, and America leads them. Railroads, steam-ships, school-houses, printing-presses, free platforms and pulpits, and open Bible, are the propelling forces of the nineteenth century.*

—Charles Carleton Coffin, *The Seat of Empire* (1870)

IN THE HISTORY OF THE UNITED STATES *the outposts of civilization have been planted, beginning with the Virginia and Massachusetts colonies and following the star of empire until they reached the Pacific Ocean. During all these days we had a frontier, a borderland between civilization and wilder-ness. The period of this frontier is rapidly passing, and when it is entirely gone the type of men it produced will be only a memory of the nation. It cannot be longer said that there is a frontier in the West. Railroads and telegraph and telephone lines cross the plains, wind through canyons and stretch over mountains, and civilization is busy building cities where once was the heart of an ancient forest, building cities where scorching sands of arid desert have been fructified by irrigation and converted into orchards and gardens.*

Up here in Northwestern Alaska is the extreme outpost of civilization in the United States. Civilization has marched westward to the Pacific, and at a single bound has gone northward beyond the Arctic Circle. We are on the frontier, but it is not like the frontier of a quarter century ago. We have brought with us the accessories of civilization. The frontiers-men were here before the discovery of gold, before we had steamship lines and telegraph and telephone lines and railroads, and burned hard coal in base burners and illuminated the darkness of the long winter nights with electric lights.

—E. S. Harrison, *Nome and Seward Peninsula* (1905)

CHAPTER I

FORGING AMERICANNESS

*Nome City was a veritable beehive of industry. It is astonishing when one
stops to think how, of a sudden, a town of five or six thousand souls sprung
into existence on this bleak and barren arctic waste. No fuel, no timber, no
food-stuffs, were there to provide the necessaries of civilization, as all were
imported from a base of supply three thousand miles distant. The general
public but faintly realize the energy and indomitable push manifest in the
upbuilding of this now world-famous town of Bering Strait.*

—George Edward Adams, *Harper's Weekly,* August 4, 1900

*To surround one's home life with the refinements and comforts of a more
easterly civilization is to express the confidence in the future that is negatived
by the uncouthness of bare walls and makeshifts, and to the extent that it is
adopted will hasten the period when Alaska shall be considered as beyond its
primary stages and its residents entitled to permanent political institutions.*

—*Council City News,* January 20, 1906

Several years before thousands of men, and a few women, went to Nome,
Alaska, on the treeless southern coast of the Seward Peninsula, one of
America's great intellectuals penned his thoughts on the concept of the
"self." A "man's Self," wrote William James, "is the sum total of all that he
can call his," including his reputation and accomplishments. If these things "wax
and prosper a man will feel triumphant," James wrote; "if they dwindle and die
away, he feels cast down."[1] James maintained that people's sense of self, or search
for such a sense, drives them to "find a home of [their] own which [they] may
live in and improve"; the search for usable selves spurs people to accumulate
property and, thus, to fortify their selves—for the loss of hard-earned property
leads to a "sense of the shrinkage of our personality."[2] James's thinking about
the self, and what people do to create identities for themselves, is a good place

to begin a discussion of early twentieth-century Nome, for when their town prospered its residents felt triumphant, when it dwindled and grew frail they felt cast down, and, despite everything, the early Nomeites who remained in their city strove to improve it. Nomeites continually looked for the next great thing.

Whether the miners, hustlers, and businessmen who went to Nome in the last years of the nineteenth century had heard of William James cannot be known. His name does not appear in any of the newspaper articles, diaries, memoirs, and letters consulted for this study. In early twentieth-century Alaska, moreover, James would have been associated with the effete East, which was scorned by Nome's rugged gold seekers, partly because of its associations with blue blood, and partly because most sentiment against the recent popular war against Spain had come from there.[3] Few of the twelve thousand people officially counted at Nome in the census of 1900 came from the eastern United States.[4]

At the same time, relative to other boomtowns in fin-de-siècle Alaska—Skagway and Dyea, for example—Nome hosted a well-informed business and merchant class;[5] the city saw the advent of impressive newspapers between 1898 and 1902; and the late-Victorian homes built there included book-filled parlors decorated with the busts of Shakespeare that were typical of the day.[6] Clichés about gold-rush Alaska's swashbuckling con artists and happy prostitutes aside,[7] many of Nome's residents were engaged readers. Indeed, the biographical sketches E. S. Harrison provides in his encyclopedic *Nome and Seward Peninsula* (1905) suggest a surprisingly well-educated population. Deemar Traphagen, for example, who became principal of the public school in Nome, had studied at the University of Michigan. J. Potter Whittren, a consulting engineer for the Council City and Solomon River Railroad, graduated from Harvard University in 1895. And P. H. Watts graduated from Miami University in 1897.[8]

Nome's challenges and hardships provided educated people with an opportunity to be philosophical. The writer Elizabeth Robins noted in her diary that a stay in Nome would give her a rare chance to study "primitive man."[9] Gold rusher Edwin Shurzer wrote in a letter home that Nome provided a person with a good opportunity to learn about human nature.[10] And by 1903, popular psychology had arrived in Nome. In June of that year one newspaper editor mused, albeit inconclusively, on the psychology of Nome. "Bleak, dreary and unforbidding [sic] the country may be," said the *Nome News* without elaboration, "but it exerts a strange psychological influence on most people that have been here."[11] So even if none of Nome's residents knew about William James's reflections on psychology, they would have understood what he had to say about the efforts people make to find and pursue plausible selves.[12] For the men and women who went to Nome gambled not only on finding gold and acquiring wealth—they were also risking their selves in a psychological sense.

In Nome at the beginning of the twentieth century we find dreams of riches dashed along with the possible selves of those who had sought new identities—as self-made men who no longer wanted to be the slaves of employers in the Outside, as engineers who could build sustainable railroads on the Seward Peninsula's spongy ground, as ordinary young men who wanted to settle down.[13] "I don't want to come home unless I can afford to get married," wrote one Nomeite who failed to meet his goal.[14] In 1900, May Fleming of Montreal intended to found a hospital at Nome. She failed, too, although she may have succeeded instead at operating a lodging house.[15]

By August of 1900 many who had gone to Nome had endured suffering and disappointment, while some who had been bent on getting rich by any means had given up. Others were disheartened that only hustlers seemed to succeed.[16] The first impression one had of summertime Nome was of chaos and filth. The city "was filled with promiscuous humanity...where the riffraff and the criminals were dumped." Not surprisingly, "[h]undreds of adventurers immediately threw up the sponge, cursed the Nome 'fake'; and if they could pay the fare, departed for home."[17]

As far as this book is concerned, fortune seekers who went to Nome and left after a few weeks or months can be placed to the side; the unrealistic possible selves they had conjured in ignorance soon evaporated. The newspaper editors who stayed at their presses did not write for the fainthearted. The commentators who declared, factually if sometimes unconvincingly, that Nome was a permanent town were not trying to rouse the spirits of the irredeemably discouraged.[18] The businessmen and homebuilders who, after 1900, demonstrated their commitment to carving Americanness into northwestern Alaska's tundra using Victorian and Edwardian designs—and by shipping wood into a nearly woodless zone—did not work for the weary who left the city when the going got tough.[19] Nomeites had said from the beginning that too many were arriving who should have stayed home.[20] As was always true—according, at least, to the trendy Social Darwinism making its rounds at the time—there were only a few who were sufficiently strong to endure drudgery and relentless challenge. Not many could lead the strenuous life promoted by the new American war hero, Theodore Roosevelt.[21] The Nomeites who stayed past the rush of 1900 believed that they could.

FORGING AMERICANNESS

In 1890 William James had made the now commonsense observation that the environment a person creates is an extension of his or her identity. We identify ourselves, for example, with the clothing we wear, and our homes become extensions of our selves.[22]

It is not surprising that turn-of-the-century Nome's residents hurried to build a city that looked much like the small American cities they had come from or had lived in before they went to Alaska.[23] To be sure, some elements of Nome's American subculture were unusual. Some Nomeites, for example, expressed the unusual view that whites were in some ways inferior to Alaska's Natives—that whites corrupted Natives.[24] This idea was partly driven by noble savage mythology (one writer called Natives "American Stone Age people"), and this provided Nomeites with a justification for separating the "races" as was typical of the American experience to that point.[25] The assumption that Alaska's Natives, devastated by imported disease, were destined for rapid extinction seems to have drawn pity from some observers who, nevertheless, clung to a socio-evolutionary creed which dictated that such was the way of the rough-and-tumble world where some kinds of humans were, naturally, more hardy than others.[26] Simultaneously, though, intermarriage and sexual relations between white men and Native women did not outrage Nome's residents. One local poet wrote openly about his "Eskimo girl" who set his heart "awhirl," and with whom he, apparently, produced "fruitage rare indeed."[27]

More striking than the differences that set Nome's subculture apart from norms in the Outside were the powerful, yet quite ordinary, ways in which the Americans in Nome asserted their cultural identity. Lawyers swarmed Nome, arguing for and against stampeding claim jumpers. (One diarist wrote that Nome's gold was locked up by litigation. Another recalled that lawyers there were "as thick as Alaska mosquitos.")[28] Literary and debating societies formed.[29] Books were in demand even among miners in the field.[30] Nomeites wanted, and received, a reliable if cumbersome mail service that kept them in touch with the Outside.[31] Middle-class, respectable residents worked to assert order in what was, through the summer of 1900, an anarchic society.[32] Nomeites informed family and friends of the modern amenities they enjoyed, such as thermometers and alarm clocks.[33] And as was trendy among New England's cultural elite, photographs of Japanese scenes found their way into at least one house in Nome.[34] At the time of the rush to Nome, a much broader craze for bicycles was underway (in 1890 some 312 firms manufactured ten million bicycles), and some of the Americans who went to Nome brought their bicycles with them, while others who did not enquired about them in letters.[35] And, as everywhere, young people in Nome got married,[36] and the beds of newlyweds squeaked in the night—in one case to the chagrin and frustration of a Victorian gentleman far from his wife but separated from vigorous youth by a mere thin wall.[37]

In the early twenty-first century, Alaskan businesses would be eager to assert a specifically Alaskan identity: The Alaska Used Computer Source, the Alaska Valuation Service, and the Great Alaska Pizza Company are among the business names entered in the 2003 edition of Anchorage's telephone book. And while Nome's businessmen soon asserted a local identity—founding, for example, the Bank of Cape Nome, the Sourdough Road House, and the Nome Drug Company—in 1900 many shops and taverns in Nome were given names that asserted their Americanness: the Alaska *and* Chicago Commercial Company, the California Bakery Café, the Golden Gate Store, the New York Kitchen, the Montana Restaurant, the California House, the Southern Saloon, the Portland.[38]

Also on display in Nome was that certain take-charge, "can-do" spirit that, for good and ill, has done so much to shape American history. "A thoroughly

Figure 5. *"Front Street," Lomen Family Collection, acc. no. 72-71-1669,*
Archives, Alaska and Polar Regions Department, University of Alaska Fairbanks.

energetic and enterprising American spirit pervades [Nome's] business world," an observer noted.[39] As was true of non-evangelical American Protestantism generally, in Nome the word *progress* had come to be synonymous with the will of Providence, which always favored material prosperity.[40] According to this creed, the faith and works of the New Testament could be transformed into "faith in our great northwestern possession" and "works in opening up . . . [Alaska's] treasury"; interior Alaska could be likened to a bright and heavenly paradise; and the merchant marine and navy could be christened "joint apostles for the greatness of the United States."[41]

And if the planting of flags indicates an assertion of national identity, then turn-of-the-century Nomeites were committed to asserting their Americanness. Even in 1899, when Nome's Front Street was essentially a tent city, its residents displayed U.S. flags. They were posted outside taverns,[42] and one visitor to Nome observed an undertaker's tent with a U.S. flag on its top.[43] An early photograph shows a group of Nomeites standing on ice, enjoying a "sourdough picnic." Incongruously, a women is holding—displaying, really—an American flag.[44] More odd is a picture of an airborne skier, a member of Nome's Ski Club, flying past an American flag planted in the snow.[45] Still another early photo reveals some nineteen American flags hanging from establishments on Nome's Front Street. The Golden Gate Hotel itself was decorated, at least temporarily, with more than fourteen American flags.[46]

On the Fourth of July flags festooned storefronts throughout boomtown Alaska, but they were usually scarce in the gateway settlements of Skagway and Dyea. Sometimes a flag was hoisted on Broadway in Skagway, sometimes it was not. Significantly, the only other flag the author found in pictures of fin-de-siècle Skagway was posted outside the *German* Bakery and Restaurant. No flags could be seen in photographs of Dyea.[47]

The Americans in Nome, who were eager to show that they could indeed Americanize the inhospitable region in which they had settled, also felt threatened—not in this case by foreigners (although that would come) but by their city's isolation and the rigors and oddity of the Seward Peninsula's environment. As the hoisting of British flags was one way Dawsonites reassured themselves of their place within the British Empire, the raising of myriad American flags in Nome bolstered the Nomeites' identity as members of a conquering people—as Americans.[48] And when, in the early 1920s, Americans from Nome unwittingly assisted an expedition to Wrangel Island to raise a British flag there, they worried that their fellow Alaskans might consider them traitors.[49]

Posting American flags everywhere was a way for Nomeites to show out-siders that their city was playing a part in American expansionism. America's culture and institutions "will follow our flag on the wings of commerce," Albert J. Beveridge said when campaigning for a seat in the Senate.[50] They may or may not have been aware of Beveridge's statement, but Nome's settlers would have agreed with it.

DAILY LIFE

Following the initial rush of 1900, Nomeites set out to create a community that was like small cities in Minnesota or Connecticut, Mississippi or Colorado. But what was hardly worth noticing in, say, San Bernardino, California, or Van Buren, Maine, was remarkable in Nome, which in the early twenty-first century remained the United States's most isolated small city. The most striking thing about Nome—particularly in an age before instant communications—is its ordi-nariness, its easily recognizable Americanness.

To be sure, Nome departed from the American norm in some respects. While Nomeites shared the prejudices of their day, enjoying, for example, a typical vaudeville show that presented "the appearance of a little darkey boy possessed of all the mischief known to the youngsters of color,"[51] it was also true that life on the Seward Peninsula was too difficult for its residents to have energy to spend on being actively contemptuous of nonwhites, particularly Natives—the most visible nonwhite population. Indeed, alongside prejudice grew up genuine interest in and even appreciation for Natives and their ways. Some Nomeites published glossaries of Native expressions to assist in conversation between Euro-Americans and Natives. Others pursued personal language study, writing Native words and phrases in their diaries for personal use. Some newcomers to the Nome region became fully conversant in Native languages. This latter group included American husbands of Inupiat women and traders who learned Inupiaq for business purposes. Meanwhile, children were encouraged to learn Native words, and some of them picked up Inupiaq while playing with Native friends. The city's high school students learned Native terms.[52]

Their proximity to Natives in a forbidding climate spurred Nomeites to forge a subculture that in some ways was unique. But the American pattern was also Nome's dominant pattern. Just as investigative journalists in the contiguous states criticized and denounced the powerful and corrupt, self-appointed muckrakers in Nome charged local politicians with rot ("The attempted graft of which I speak was in connection with the proposed purchase of the Staples building and several members of the [city] council were to have participated").[53] As happened in the States, independent labor in Nome was soon superseded by corporate labor and, consequently, unionized employees used work stoppages to extract better deals from employers.[54] In 1906 Upton Sinclair's novel *The Jungle* introduced American readers to the wretchedly unhealthy conditions in the country's meat industry, and, in the same year, Nomeites were informed that A.B.C. "Bohemian Beer" of St. Louis was brewed in meticulously cleaned facilities.[55] Heightened health standards enjoyed in Chicago and San Francisco were also appreciated in Nome.

In the Outside, increasing numbers of Americans with disposable income could buy "ventilated health underwear" and doctor-recommended "invigorator corsets." Nomeites, too, could take their extra money to the Simpson Brothers store to buy stylish nightgowns ($1.00) or raccoon coats ($42.50) or kimonos (85¢).[56] For $4.00 they could purchase a ten-pound tin of coffee, America's hot beverage of choice since the colonial revolt against English tea.[57] In November of 1906, goods available to Floridians and Los Angelenos—coconuts, oranges, and olives—were available at the Snake River Grocery. The next month Archer, Ewing and Co. touted its commercial strength in the face of ice-bound competition, advertising, among other things, its strawberries, apricots, and apples.[58] Nome's popular culture was also thoroughly ordinary. In the fall of 1906 about two thousand phonograph records were available at the Nome Bazaar—among them "A Monkey on a String," "The Goo Goo Man," "My Creole Sue," and "Hear Dem Bells."

At the same time President Roosevelt promoted the strenuous life, the *Nome Daily Gold Digger* observed that in the wintry Seward Peninsula—as in Seattle, as in Milwaukee, as in New Orleans—the man who "greases the wheels of progress and keeps the world spinning round" is of great value, while "chronic kickers and chronic knockers" should be ignored.[59] While New York governor Charles Seymour Whitman invited laborers to jump heartily into the drama of American life, a prominent Nomeite praised "a frontier camp like this, where a man's chances are *great*, where there is *freedom* and *life* and 'something doing.'"[60] At a time of unprecedented levels of immigration, many Americans on the East and West Coasts denounced hyphenated Americanism and declared that all Americans' allegiance must be to the United States alone. Nomeites, too, believed that immigrants unhappy with their new country—the U.S. in general or Alaska in particular—should pack their bags and go.[61]

America's big-city newspapers—most famously Joseph Pulitzer's *New York World* and William Randolph Hearst's *Evening Journal*—waged war against one another, as did Nome's. In retaliation for attacks against him, S. H. Stevens of the *Daily Gold Digger* (and future governor of Alaska) reported that earlier in life Harry Steel—or "Harry Steal," editor of the "try-weakly" (i.e., tri-weekly) *Nome Nugget*—had been fired from a government job. The *Gold Digger* also wondered if Steel took illicit drugs.[62] Indeed, "the people of Nome, or rather those who have lived here since 1900," the newspaper declared

> know almost to a detail of the disgustingly immoral and dissolute life led by Harry Steal [*sic*], since his first arrival here till the present day.... The community knows how he has retrograded and degenerated down the line, from the time of his unsavory connection with Vivian Carlyle, who was tried in the district court three times for smoking opium, up until a week ago when he made a disgusting exhibition of himself at a public dance by appearing in such a driveling and drunken condition that the very sight of him was nauseating to a respectable woman.[63]

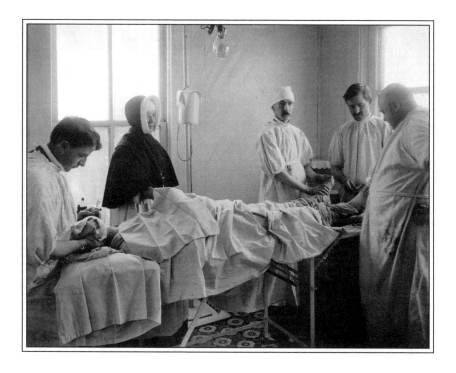

FIGURE 6. *"Operating Room," Elizabeth Wood Collection, acc. no. 2000-101-302, Archives, Alaska and Polar Regions Department, University of Alaska Fairbanks.*

In this one passage we see exemplified the kind of yellow journalism that came into prominence in the early twentieth century; we scent the popular scandal-mongering—such as troubled Grover Cleveland's presidential election of 1888—of an increasingly prosperous American public; we learn about the anxiety of a narcotic trafficked from Asia, into which American empire had spread; and we divine a Victorian sense of moral rectitude, such as would lead to prohibition in Alaska in 1918. Who can doubt that middle-American culture had taken deep root in the Nome region's tundra?

But neither scandal nor political argument was what most struck visitors to Nome. In 1908 the travel writer Ella Higginson noted that Nome was wonderful and picturesque; it took an indefinable hold on people who visited it. "In many ways Nome is the most interesting place in Alaska," Higginson continued. "Treeless and harborless it began and has continued, surmounting all obstacles that lay in the way of its becoming a city." Higginson was amazed by how ordinary Nome was.

> It has a water system.... It has a wireless telegraph station, a telephone service, and electric light plant.... There are three good newspapers...three banks...two good public schools; three churches; hospitals.... The orders of Masons, Odd Fellows, Knights of Pythias, Eagles, and Arctic Brotherhood have clubs at Nome.... [T]he wives of [the Arctic Brotherhood's] members form the most exclusive society of the North.[64]

Higginson did not mention the Elks Club or the Nome Athletic Club or the Nome Gun Club, which, like those she did notice, had been established several years before.[65] She did not mention the Sons of the North, the Knights of Robert Emmet, or the women's organization Kegoyah Kozga, all of which fostered a sense of community and offered entertainment—tug-of-war contests, music concerts, festivals, public lectures, and plays.[66] She did not mention that Nome's politically minded residents could ally themselves with local Democrats, socialists, or the Nome Republican Committee, or even the Nome Non-Partisan Political Committee.[67]

What Higginson did make clear is that the Nomeites who had stayed after the stampede of 1900 had succeeded in what they had set out to do. They had planted an easily identifiable American community in a most daunting environment.

CHAPTER 2

REACHING FOR EMPIRE

We [Americans] are now twenty millions strong; and how long . . . will it take to cover the continent with our posterity, from the Isthmus of Darien to Behring's straits?

—U.S. Representative Andrew Kennedy, 1846[1]

The sturdy men and women who conquered the great Northwest, who pierced the back-bone of the continent with railway tunnels, who made productive millions of acres of desert land, were of the same hardy stock who, to-day, by their endurance, energy and industry are slowly converting the vast wilderness of Alaska into an Empire.

—John Underwood, *Alaska: An Empire in the Making*, 1912

Historian Stephen Haycox is correct in saying that "[m]ost Alaskans have been willing to stay in the territory only if they could enjoy the amenities and comforts of modern American culture," and that Americans went to Alaska for wealth.[2] But many who went to Nome, and elsewhere in the Seward Peninsula, at the beginning of the twentieth century also wanted to take on a greater challenge. They wanted to see if they could conquer and domesticate that most formidable of wildernesses.[3]

For more than two centuries before the gold rush in Nome—from the time when Puritan divines sermonized that Americans, like the ancient Israelites before them, had a divine obligation to possess the New World—Americans had moved westward with a sense of mission and purpose. They talked and acted as if they were building a Promised Land.[4] By 1900, the term most associated with this cause—"manifest destiny"—had been in use for over fifty years. It was the Americans' manifest destiny, wrote the journalist John O'Sullivan, "to overspread the continent allotted by Providence for the free developing of our yearly multiplying millions."[5] Now, to some at the end of the nineteenth

century, the occupation and exploitation of Alaska seemed a logical next step
in the Anglo-Saxon march across the continent.[6] It comes as no surprise, then,
that the Monroe Doctrine, along with Theodore Roosevelt's imperialistic ventures in Asia and Latin America, received positive notice in Nome's newspapers.
Meanwhile, at least one U.S. Senator, George Turner of Washington, thought
that more than a hundred thousand colonists would soon leave the contiguous
states for Alaska and British Columbia, the latter of which, according to the
prevalent American view, would soon be annexed to the United States.[7] Eight
years later, the *Nome Daily Gold Digger* raised Turner's figure to millions.[8]

So Nome was founded at a time of lofty nationalism and imperial grasping.
Just thirty years earlier, northern industrial nationalism had triumphed in the
Civil War over a more agrarian southern nationalism—and, perhaps significantly, few representatives of the vanquished Confederacy found their way to
Nome.[9] And even as Americans began to travel to Nome, the United States was
busy consolidating its new empire—the fruit, in Secretary of State John Hay's
words, of a "splendid little war" against Spain, along with the machinations of
sugar monopolists in Hawai'i. At the same time, major American politicians
assumed that it was only a matter of time until the United States absorbed
Canada. "The common interest of Canada, of the United States and of Great
Britain would be served by Canadian annexation," observed the *Fort Wrangel
News*.[10] Partly in response to this American threat and to the energy driving
the rapidly growing British Empire, Canadian nationalism was also on the rise.
Late-nineteenth-century English-speaking Canadians were busy possessing their
own western land, while francophones in Quebec were occupying land once
inhabited primarily by English speakers.[11]

Everywhere one looked in North America, in other words, the civilized were,
to use the phraseology of biblical motifs popular at the time,[12] taking dominion over the earth and making gardens of wildernesses.[13] Former Confederate
vice president Alexander Stephens had said that Alaska's snowbound wilderness
could never be made into a habitable place.[14] Some set out to prove him wrong.
"[We] open our eyes in a land as yet only spoken of and but little known,"
declared one Alaskan newspaper in 1887, "but in a land that will emanate from
wilderness into one of the richest sections of the globe."[15] Eleven years later,
this theme remained strong. Skagway, said one editor, had wrenched a thriving,
marvelous city from a howling wilderness.[16] In 1903 the *Nome News* suggested
that a way to tame the Alaskan wilderness would be for Americans to build a
prestige-enhancing railroad that would make it possible to travel in a Pullman

car from New York to Nome.[17] Word of this bold scheme spread across the country, even to the Franco-Americans of northern Maine.[18]

But could these Americans really take dominion on the land surrounding Cape Nome? Could they possess the forbidding Seward Peninsula? Could these Americans overcome the challenges of this climate the way their counterparts had proven their mastery in the tropical climates of Hawai'i and the South Pacific? This was a new challenge. No large group of Americans had tried to possess a land like this, where residents were almost completely cut off from the Outside for more than half the year, where the sight of the first ship to make it into port each spring was met with daylong church bell ringing, where no trees grew.[19] The late-nineteenth-century cartoonist Thomas Nast lampooned Alaska as little more than icebergs and polar bears.[20] The joke did not apply to southeastern Alaska, which enjoyed moderate weather and year-round access to the sea and to ports in the contiguous American states through the year.[21] But Nast's caricature *did* fit Nome; it *was* an "icebox" for more than half the year. Nome

FIGURE 7. *"Nome 1907," Lomen Family Collection, acc. no. 72-71-1697N, Archives, Alaska and Polar Regions Department, University of Alaska Fairbanks.*

was a "weird country"[22] where the ground remained frozen through summer. In April of 1900 Nomeites read that the *New Orleans Times-Democrat* had called their city "the most remote and isolated mining camp in North America."[23] In May the *Seattle Post-Intelligencer* remarked that Nome was the "strangest community ever seen upon the face of this old earth."[24] These external views echoed what the residents of Nome already knew. "Perhaps nowhere on the globe is there another cosmopolitan community so shut in and alone, as we are here in the Arctic," declared the *Nome Gold Digger* in November of 1899.[25] "On the face of the globe there will probably be no large community of civilized men and women so completely isolated as this for the next seven or eight months."[26]

Of course, it was possible that, in the race to prove one's mettle, Nome's isolation in the far north could work to a person's advantage. An intellectual fashion of the time among Anglo-Canadian nationalists and some Americans dictated that northerners who lived out their days in cold and harsh climates were congenitally more industrious and individualistic, philosophically deeper, and physically, morally, politically, and spiritually superior to people from more tropical climes, who inclined toward degeneracy and effeminacy.[27] Fred Lockley, who went to Nome in 1900, wondered if he had been drawn there by inclinations bequeathed to him by a remote ancestor, "some hardy Norseman or adventurous Viking."[28] With self-serving approval, Nome's newspapers noticed the sturdy Norsemen inhabiting Iceland, whose latitude was the same as that of the Seward Peninsula.[29] And a perusal of the newspapers published at the time in Nome, as well as of contemporary Alaskan writing, suggests that stolid endurance through the winter was considered, and remains, a key Alaskan trait.[30] If Nomeites were to tame this wilderness, as Americans had tamed myriad wildernesses before, they would have to make a virtue of living with cold, isolation, and darkness.

An axiom of psychology is that claims of superiority often mask feelings of inferiority, and aspirations to high position were easy to come by in late-nineteenth-century North America. In the late nineteenth century, Franco-Canadians, who were increasingly outnumbered in Canada, boasted of their status as a divinely chosen people,[31] while English-speaking Canadians, feeling steadily weaker in the face of an expanding United States, reveled in their moral superiority.[32] The United States—in 1898 a new kid on the imperial block—radiated bravado: the public was eager to smash Spain; and Teddy Roosevelt, the assistant secretary of the navy when war was declared, had earlier stated his desire for the U.S. simply to go to war—any foe would do.[33]

This spirit was of one substance but it had many faces, and it made Alaskans eager to claim that their cities and towns were at the cutting edge of national and imperial significance. Skagway's boosters called their settlement a "city of destiny"; it was to Juneau's jealous inhabitants "what the proverbial red flag is to a bull."

> The bare mention of the name Skagway sets the average Juneauite wild, not with an honest spirit of business rivalry, but with a small, petty, envious feeling akin to the mean jealousy of a dyspeptic dwarf at the overtowering size of a well-formed man."[34]

Dyea, too, was prepared to outperform all competitors. "It will be the seaport of the gold fields, the greatest outfitting center in America, a mining point of importance—the metropolis, in fact, of the northern wonderland."[35]

On the Seward Peninsula, meantime, Teller promised to rival Nome in size and wealth, ultimately becoming the "Queen city of the ice."[36] In turn, Nome's newspapers saw nothing to fear from Port Clarence or St. Michael.[37] And so the quest for dominance went:

> Here [in Nome] empire grand will quick expand
> Great factories build, with workmen filled....
> This burg of Nome will rival Rome....
> We'll gain renown as a red-hot town
> And gold galore from Bering's shore
> Will give us mirth—we'll own the earth.[38]

This stanza, extracted from a typically abysmal poem by the miner T. F. Kane and published in the *Nome Gold Digger*, shows that newspaper commentary in Nome could rise to the level of hype issued by southeastern Alaskan enthusiasts. One might have thought that the Seward Peninsula's isolation through much of the year would have led Nome's promoters to have a firmer grasp on what was possible. And, in time, this elevated sense of expectation would give way to more subdued language (most of the time). But in 1899 a writer *could* say that Nome was the center of the arctic gold country toward which the eyes of the world were turned. And given the figures of speech of the day, a Nome editorialist could declare without embarrassment that the gold flowing from Nome, "the Golden Queen of the Bering Sea," would strengthen "the giant infant among the world's nations," the United States.[39] Indeed, the gold extracted from the Seward Peninsula helped to push Congress to pass the Gold

Standard Act of 1900, which put an end to the Populists' movement for the monetization of silver.[40]

Behind the inflated language coming out of Nome was the belief, or the hope, that there was no foreseeable end to the gold stored on the beaches and in the rivers and ground near the city. Nome would not have existed at all were it not for gold. But for some in the city—for those concerned about its permanence—there was the hope that Nome would play an important role in the expansion of the American empire.

News from the Outside did not take up much space in Nome's newspapers in the first years of the twentieth century, even in the summer when papers from beyond Alaska were available. The preponderance of Outside news printed in Nome's newspapers involved U.S.–Asia relations and American and European imperial adventures and expansionism. Readers of the May 21, 1900, edition of the *Gold Digger*, for example, saw front-page headlines about

FIGURE 8. *"Teacher," Elizabeth Wood Collection, acc. no. 2000-101-272, Archives, Alaska and Polar Regions Department, University of Alaska Fairbanks.*

Spanish-American War hero Admiral Dewey's intention to run for president (he ended up not running), new legislation for Puerto Rico, the whereabouts of military leaders in the Philippines, and Japanese laborers "pouring into coast cities by the thousands." These stories reflect the fact that, between 1898 and the first years of the twentieth century, foreign affairs dominated American news. But the studied focus on such news in Nome's newspapers also indicates that, to a considerable extent, the eyes of Nome's settled residents looked outward—to the world outside, but also to their own future.

Accordingly, Nomeites' public words frequently asserted their city's Americanness by placing it within an imperial context or by associating it with images of victorious Anglo-Saxondom, and observers saw that Nome was infused with the energetic and enterprising spirit of Anglo-Saxons.[41] One writer reported on a "fleet larger than the British used in their war with South Africa [riding] at anchor in these northern waters." T. F. Kane mused that the American flag waved proudly and freely over both the icebergs of the far north and the "fragrant isles of Philippines."[42] General textbooks for American children published around the turn of the century placed Alaska within the broadened context of American empire and commercial expansion.[43]

For a period, then, there was reason for Nomeites to think that Alaska in general and Nome in particular could—*would*— play an important role in expanding American empire. After all, one of Secretary of State William Seward's intentions when he orchestrated the purchase of Alaska from Russia in 1867 had been to make Alaska the drawbridge between North America and Asia. Seward, like others, believed that control of the Pacific would ensure the political and commercial control of the globe.[44] Well before the Spanish-American War, Alaskan editors assumed that their readers wanted to know about American activities in the Pacific, publishing, for example, lengthy articles on Hawai'ian affairs.[45]

Accordingly, by the end of the 1890s many Nomeites and visitors to Nome assumed that Alaska would be closely linked to the growing Asian trade. "Dutch Harbor will very probably become an important station in the Philippine and Asiatic trade" of the United States, wrote one memoirist.[46] Others spoke of a proposed bridge that would connect the Aleutian Islands with Asia.[47] "Naturally California, [Washington], and Alaska will be far more largely benefited by the opening up of Oriental markets than any other section of the Union," claimed Juneau's *Alaska Miner*.[48]

The *Miner* and other Alaskan newspapers could not help but notice that the United States' economic interests in Asia had expanded dramatically.[49] The value of American exports to China stood at about $4 million in 1892 and at $11.9 million in 1897. In 1900 the *Gold Digger* observed that San Francisco had gathered $7 million in trade from the Philippines.[50] And following a visit from a Japanese envoy to Skagway in 1898, the *Daily Alaskan* promised a Japanese steamship line to that port in the near future.[51] Peter Bayne, an early settler with little faith in the durability of Nome, was nevertheless optimistic that on the Seward Peninsula there would be a city from which large ocean steamers and railroads would come and go. "The forces are surely working, and the time is not remote."[52] Of course, Nome's newspapers, like Alaskan papers generally, supported America's Open Door policy in China.[53]

Clearly, Nomeites saw Alaska generally, and their city in particular, in the context of expanding American empire. The Reynolds–Alaska Company, with interests in south Alaska, promoted the district as the "Keystone of American Supremacy on the Pacific Ocean."[54] The *Nome News* made the point this way:

> Alaska's long seacoast, stretching through 30 degrees of longitude and 20 degrees of latitude, embracing 26,000 linear miles of water frontage, offers the greatest opportunities for commerce. This, with the seacoast from San Diego to Puget Sound makes no question of the nation's supremacy on the Pacific.... *Potentially Alaska is an empire in wealth*, and before this generation passes away, from an industrial point of view, it will be one of the most noted parts of American territory.[55]

Observers in Seattle saw much the same thing,[56] as did levelheaded government agents who argued for the future importance of the Seward Peninsula's Port Clarence. "It takes no very vivid imagination to foresee that the time is not far off when many thriving towns will line the shores on the Alaskan as well as the Siberian side of the [Bering] sea," wrote Joseph Evans, an agent for the Treasury Department; "when imports and exports will cross the straits back and forth in numberless vessels to supply busy marts; when in fact the [Behring] Sea will become a great American Baltic."[57]

Evans, whose work was praised by, among others, Alaska governor John Brady, went on to suggest that since the Seward Peninsula was destined to become a key link in the United States' expanding commercial empire, the government should establish facilities there before many more hardy pioneers arrived.[58] Governor Brady also saw Alaska's strategic importance in the global competition for trade with Asia and suggested that railroads should be built in Alaska to allow eager Americans to occupy the territory and make it fruitful for the good of the nation and its expanding trade.[59] Nomeites wanted to be a part of this American "progress that seems of divine appointment." If they could do so, they would have good reason to be proud that they were Americans.[60] In January 1900, Dr. L. L. Wirt preached at Nome's St. Bernard chapel, urging his hearers to put off all that would stand in the way of progress, religiously, morally, economically, and, thus, imperially.

One thing Nome could do toward that end would be to raise a company or regiment to be sent to China to "assist in wreaking vengeance upon the [Boxer Rebellion's] yellow skinned murderers of the innocent foreigners."[61] Nome could also promote American influence and further the cause of progress by serving as a rail link between the U.S. and Russia in an envisioned railroad stretching from New York to St. Petersburg, and thence to Western Europe. "Yes, the road will be built," said one booster. "I may not live to see it done," he continued, echoing Moses who foresaw a promised land he himself would not arrive at, but "[s]cience is accomplishing many things, and by the aid of electricity we may yet be whisked off from New York to St. Petersburg at the rate of 200 miles an hour."[62] If the Alaska–Siberia road was built, the *Gold Digger* noted in 1899, it would do an enormous business, so Nomeites hoped it would be built.[63] Their hope was spurred by publications with titles like William Gilpin's *Cosmopolitan Railway Compacting and Fusing Together All the World's Continents* (1890) and Harry DeWindt's *Through the Gold Fields of Alaska and Bering Straits* (1899). Even before the railroad was built, Nomeites claimed that they could provide an example of advanced civilization to Siberia and be a source of supplies to eastern Russia.[64] And by 1905—the same year work began on an improbable railroad connecting Miami to Key West, and not long after capitalists conjured a railroad connecting Hudson Bay to Buenos Aires—Nomeites were traveling as tourists to Siberia, where natives were reported to have gathered gladly around the American flag.[65] Two years later, with the Seward Peninsula's own projects in mind, the *Gold Digger* noticed that the completed Miami–Key West railroad was a marvel.[66]

Related to the Nomeites' expansive vision was the feeling that the city could serve American expansion by being a port of entry into the United States[67] and, like other cities in Alaska, possibly hosting naval vessels from which American power could be projected.[68] U.S. government marine services had long been a presence in Alaska, maintaining order, enforcing laws, rescuing sailors in distress, and protecting American resources from foreigners, particularly the Japanese and Russians.[69] But, on the heels of the U.S. Navy's exploits in the

Spanish-American War, and for several years thereafter, it seemed that a more imperially oriented naval presence in Alaska was in order.[70]

THWARTED AMBITION

All of these aspirations were thwarted.[71] Over one hundred of Nome's men volunteered to help put the Boxer Rebellion down, but Governor Brady declined their offer.[72] For practical reasons—cost, the instability of tundra, the refusal of the Russian and American governments to approve and fund the scheme, and, after 1910, declining interest and a shrinking population in the Seward Peninsula—no railroad connecting Nome to the contiguous American states or Alaska to Siberia was built.[73] Indeed, by 1905 Nomeites had seen several much more reasonable railroad plans come and go. Some of the seemingly practical schemes they heard about—schemes promoted by the knowledgeable and reasonable[74]—never materialized. The Council City and Solomon River Railroad, also called the North Star Line, never reached Council City, and by 1908 it was defunct. The Wild Goose Railroad—"Hardly more than a trolley," and reorganized in 1903 as the Nome Arctic Railroad—took Nomeites to Anvil Creek, but only until 1905, when it ceased operations.[75] The Bering Sea Council City Railroad never had a single customer. Neither did the Bering Strait Railroad Company, or the Tin City and Arctic Railroad Company, or the Alaska Coast Line Railroad Company.[76] In early 1907 an editorial in the *Gold Digger* called for government assistance in building railroads in Alaska generally, although the article never mentioned Nome or the Seward Peninsula.[77] By that time Nomeites had replaced hopes for an enduring railroad that would connect them to the outside with calls for sled trails that would improve mail service in winter.[78]

As for a naval base, the U.S. Navy did plan to build one in Alaska in 1900, but that would not actually happen until 1911,[79] well after it had become clear that Nome would not be closely linked with U.S.–Asia trade. And, in any case, there is no evidence that the navy ever considered northwest Alaska as an early twentieth-century base of operations. In January of 1905 Governor Brady requested that two gunboats be ordered to cruise the Alaskan coast continually. This would help to keep Natives and "unruly whites" in order, Brady wrote. It would also serve to acquaint young navy officers with Alaska's ports and strategic points—knowledge that would be invaluable in case the U.S. went to war with Japan. Secretary of the Navy Paul Morton brushed off Brady's request in a single, albeit lengthy, sentence.[80] (In the same year, however, Secretary of War William Taft wrote that the telegraph and cable lines that connected Nome to Valdez and thence to the contiguous states had obvious strategic importance.)[81]

In the early years, Nome was also passed over as an official American port of entry. "So far no evidence has been presented tending to show that Nome has a good harbor, and suitable shipping facilities are necessary for a port of entry," said Treasury Department agent Evans on a fact-finding mission in Nome. "The second question we have been considering," Evans continued, "is the lasting nature of Nome. A custom house must be a permanent institution, not a floating affair, like a camp meeting."[82] Four weeks earlier, on May 1, 1900, Evans had been more straightforward with Lyman Gage, the Secretary of the Treasury. "My inquiry forces me to the conclusion that no good reason exists at present for establishing a sub-port at Cape Nome," he wrote. "Although there are fully two

FIGURE 9. *"Seward Peninsula Railroad," Elizabeth Wood Collection, acc. no. 2000-101-305, Archives, Alaska and Polar Regions Department, University of Alaska Fairbanks.*

thousand people wintering at Nome, it must nevertheless be regarded at present as a temporary mining camp."[83] Six months later Evans would close the book, writing that losses to shipping and human life at Nome, where there was no harbor, had ended consideration of a proposition to create a port of entry there. Evans' assistant, Revenue Cutter Service agent D. H. Jarvis, who was stationed in Nome, agreed with this assessment.[84] Neither man, in fact, seemed to hold the city of Nome, as opposed to the Seward Peninsula generally, in high esteem. This may have been because of Nome's forbidding geographical location, which had been commented on by government inspectors before.[85] Or perhaps the rowdiness and dirtiness of the place in its early days soured them.

When the U.S. government's deputy collector of customs at Nome requested a salary of $2400, an understandable sum given the cost of living there, Jarvis instead recommended $2000 in light of the comparative unimportance of the work to be done there.[86] (At the same time, Jarvis informed the Secretary of the Treasury that Teller City and Port Clarence would be of "much importance.") And while in late 1901 most of Evans' subordinates in ports throughout Alaska were considered by him to be excellent or very good, the Treasury Department had assigned a new agent to Nome who was, for the time at least, "useless."[87] Soon thereafter Evans determined that Nome's customs affairs would be supervised by the Treasury Department's agent, J. H. Causten, who was based at St. Michael.[88]

The news that Nome would not become a port of entry came as a blow, not only in what it portended for the city's economy, but because, between 1898 and 1903, port status for Alaskan towns seemed to promise not only potential wealth but stability, or, at a minimum, victory in the struggle for municipal prestige. When San Francisco's Chamber of Commerce passed a resolution calling the potential establishment of a port at Nome a menace to the interests of "the Pacific Coast and, indirectly, to those of the whole country," it was obviously defending local ambitions.[89] Newspaper editors could boost their towns vigorously, but decisions about where official ports and subports in Alaska would be were in the hands of Evans and his colleagues. St. Michael, they believed, was an important subport, so it remained open. The subports at Circle City and Unga, on the other hand, were closed and moved, respectively, to Eagle City and Sand Point. In 1900, Treasury revived a port at Dutch Harbor while it closed another at Mary Island.[90] A rumor that the port at Ketchikan was to be moved sparked a letter campaign that spurred congressmen to rally for its survival.[91]

Port status indicated *recognition*. Ports were a mark of success—at least temporarily, for competitors could knock a town off its pedestal. The language, sarcastic and dismissive, employed by Evans in a letter not meant for public consumption provides one with a feel for the competitive spirit at work among Alaska's boomtowns. "Dyea has been swallowed up by Skagway," he wrote,

> a young ravenous and remorseless monster, the largest in this great domain, that has squatted itself in the valley at the head of the Lynn Canal, and firmly clutched his iron claws into the shelving rocks on the adjacent mountain sides to stay for all time, and with open maw to exact tribute from traders from far and near as they pass to and from beyond the great valley of the Yukon. Trade from Dyea is gone. Gone are the people who lived there. Nothing remains but empty cabins, hungry ravens, silence and desolation. Even her giant tramway that used to groan and creak under heavy dead and living freight, has crawled over the mountain out of sight, as though broken hearted that the fickle jade of commerce had deserted and joined a more vigorous lusty companionship.[92]

To gain and lose a port—to gain and lose status—as Dyea had done was bad. But at this moment, Nome would not get a port at all.[93]

In his first lengthy memorandum on Nome to the Secretary of the Treasury, Evans wrote that no inconvenience or hardship would come to the trade and welfare of the Nome region if a port of entry were not established there.[94] But, at the least, Evans' conclusion would strike a psychological blow. The *Gold Digger* gave the story the defensive headline "Against this Place."[95] And for Nomeites there were Evans' unpleasant words to consider. "A custom house must be a permanent institution," he had said, "not a floating affair, like a camp meeting."[96] Early twentieth-century Americans knew that religious camp meetings stirred temporary enthusiasm and operated beyond the norms of day-to-day life. And Nomeites, who had seen ships come and go, knew that floating things were often fleeting things.

In 1900 one scheme aimed at compensating for the lack of a harbor called for the building of a deepwater pier that would extend a mile out to sea, where oceangoing vessels could discharge cargo.[97] This idea came to nothing. Three years later, the *Nome Nugget* hopefully but incorrectly reported that the city was again on the point of becoming a port of entry, an event that would be a boon to its public life.[98] A few months later, disappointed again, the *Nome News* decried the city's "unfortunate location" upon "a treacherous and storm-swept coast" and called for the development of harbor facilities which would allow the city to become a port of entry and thus maintain and enhance Nome's status.[99]

It was, perhaps, a sneaking anxiety that caused the *Nome News* to declare in 1903 that among "the *probabilities* of the near future is a railroad line passing through a tunnel *under* [the] Bering straits."[100] To a point, the *News* was only reporting; there *was* a plan afoot—yet another plan—for the Alaska Short Line Railway and Navigation Company to link up with the Trans-Siberian Railroad and tie the continents together. Among the scheme's early supporters were a former governor of Iowa and the founder of the bank of San Francisco.[101] Writing for the *Review of Reviews* in 1902, Herman Rosenthal asserted that building railroads that connected the U.S. to Russia and Japan would involve "no greater difficulties than were encountered in the construction of the existing transcontinental railroads."[102] (In 2003, the Bering Strait Tunnel and Railroad Group would seek political and financial support to do a comparable thing.)[103] But like the rest of the schemes in which Nomeites invested the hope that their town would be linked with international trade and American expansion, this one fell through.[104]

By the summer of 1905, the claim that the dredging of a harbor at the mouth of the Snake River would "result in placing Nome in the position of a true metropolis" had a dead ring to it.[105] So did the *Gold Digger*'s report two years later that a large harbor that could accommodate "coasting vessels" and, possibly, ocean steamers was in the works.[106] Nothing would come of these plans for some fifteen years, and dredging at the mouth of the Snake River would prove impractical for a long time to come.[107]

Indeed, as early as the end of 1902 it seemed to some that Nome's boom days had passed.[108] There was much gold yet to be taken from the country, but this would be done primarily by machines owned by corporations that employed relatively few men.[109]

ALASKAN IDENTITY

Along with the realization that most of what Alaska's boomtowns had gained for themselves would be lost and that Alaska would not play a significant role in the early growth of American expansion came an increasing sense of Alaskan identity. As the philosopher William James might have said at the time,[110] the "possible selves" some Nomeites had pursued, or had hoped for—as important players within the American empire—were exchanged for another identity: Alaskan. In the transition, some linked the two possibilities, claiming that "Alaska is an empire itself."[111] And as the first years of the twentieth century passed, easy approval of American empire among Nomeites faded. On the Fourth of July in 1900, Nomeites had asserted their American identity by festooning their town with flags and organizing patriotic parades. On 1905, the Fourth was met with "no preparations...to observe the day."[112]

Americans who had gone to Alaska and stayed there remained American, of course, but they came to see themselves as Americans of a special kind.[113] This was spurred by the conclusion that Alaskans inhabited a fringe easily ignored or mistreated by the federal government.[114] Their belief was incorrect. Government agents had established law and order, set up a school, planted telegraph wires and cables, and built a court and a prison, among many other things.[115] But some real desires went unfulfilled, and the challenges Nomeites faced made them feel as if they were alone in the world. "The time will come when all federal officials in Alaska will be appointed from Alaska and because they are Alaskans," the *Nome Nugget* claimed:

> Alaska will, in time, work out her own salvation. It will take time but it will come. The federal government and congress we may be sure, are not lying awake o' nights pondering over the fate of this territory.[116]

Meanwhile, Skagway's *Daily Alaskan* entertained thoughts of secession. In a Republic of Alaska, that paper suggested, the needs of Alaskans would not be ignored.[117] This sentiment was repeated through the first years of the twentieth century. Others in southeastern Alaska continued to contemplate annexation to Canada.[118] The *Nome Nugget* rejected such talk but saw that it pointed to the spirit of Alaska's Americans who had grown disgusted by the federal government's neglect.[119]

For a while, then, Nomeites had believed that American empire provided them with a grand opportunity. Then they came to believe that empire had passed them by. This realization was more difficult to accept, given the norms of the day, because nonwhites within the empire seemed to get preferential treatment from the government. The government "gives to Hawaii a delegate in congress, but it refuses to permit a larger white community on this continent to have any representatives in its deliberations," the *Nome News* complained.[120] Three years later the *Nugget* observed that Alaska contributed greater wealth to the United States than the Philippines, yet Filipinos received better treatment from the federal government. "In the eyes of the prophylactic congress [*sic*] of the United States, one brown Filipino is better than fifty thousand white Alaskans."[121] The government seemed glad to build railroads for poor, uneducated Filipinos while Alaskans had to fend for themselves.[122] Such were the observations of people who believed that their grand project had failed.

But the story does not end here. As we shall see in the next chapter, Nome's citizens proved Joseph Evans wrong. Nome would outperform both Teller (near Port Clarence) and St. Michael.[123] In the face of difficulty and against the heavy words of doubters, Nomeites had asserted their American identity and built an enduring American subculture on the tundra. They had possessed the land. They had turned their arctic wilderness into an early twentieth-century American outpost. They had played an important, if necessarily peripheral, role in American expansion.

CHAPTER 3

WINNING

There are years and years of work left in the hills of Seward Peninsula,
and that generations of men will continue the great industry of mining
in this country is the prophecy of scientific and practical men who have
knowledge of the land's worth.

—*Nome Daily Gold Digger*, December 30, 1907

[It] was a pleasant little shock to see the evidence of modern industry and
to be made aware of this brave little community of adventurers so far from
civilization.

—T. A. Rickard, *Through the Yukon and Alaska*, 1909

In an imperial age, the Seward Peninsula's residents and visitors appropriated the language of empire. Writing for *National Geographic*, Captain George S. Gibbs referred to the rich heart of the empire developing in Alaska.[1] Another observer called Alaska a "northern empire of stupendous mineral resources."[2] A government surveyor asserted that Finland was a barren waste compared to the agricultural potential of the Alaskan empire.[3]

Accordingly, as the first decade of the twentieth century wore on, Alaskans continued to look outward for signs of what was on their own horizon. If the focus of newspaper articles can be taken as a measure of public interest, they paid attention especially to China, Japan, and Russia—nations involved, in one way or another, in the growth of empires. Nomeites read that the Russians and Chinese were on the verge of war, that Russia had its greedy eyes on British India (a long-standing concern),[4] that Russian officials had cut down American flags in New Chwang (Manchuria), and that Russia had plans to improve the Trans-Siberian Railway.[5] Nomeites wondered when the U.S. government would begin to appreciate the Seward Peninsula's strategic importance.

In 1905 "much indignation" was aroused when a Russian Orthodox bishop ministering to Natives in Sitka planted a Russian flag next to an American one outside his mission church. An official at the Department of the Interior wrote that Alaska's governor John Brady should make it clear to the bishop that "the guaranteed freedom of worship of the Greek Church [sic] in Alaska is limited to its religious functions, and cannot include the semi-political features suggested by the display of a foreign flag."[6]

And in Alaska, as elsewhere, Japanese immigration to the west coasts of the U.S. and Canada, along with the accompanying fear of the "yellow peril," led to war talk—even as the Canadian, U.S., and Japanese governments were working on arriving at immigration-restricting "gentlemen's agreements."[7] In their newspapers Nomeites read that Japan had borrowed money from France in preparation for combat. At the same time, America's Pacific and Asian fleets were undergoing reform, although the government denied that this had anything to do with military plans. Nomeites knew that Senator George Perkins of California had said that Japan wished to colonize the United States, and a rumor that Fort Davis, three miles east of Nome, had been told to get ready for inevitable war made its rounds.[8] "Today an urgent order was given to all stations along both the Atlantic and Pacific coasts to practice repelling invaders," the Nugget reported.

> Nome might well look ahead to what might happen to it in the event of war with Japan. The Japanese have always looked with a covetous eye on this region.... In the event of a war a Japanese cruiser might easily sail into Nome harbor some day ... hold up the shipping, land a strong body of troops, and under cover of quick-firing guns sail away with the whole result of the winter's clean-up. What is to prevent such a performance? The few troops at Fort Davis would be helpless. The citizens could do nothing.

In late 1907, the Gold Digger reported that about three dozen young men, stalwart and strong, had organized themselves into a home guard for Nome's protection.[9] Yes, Fort Davis was nearby, but Nomeites had come to doubt that the federal government would protect them.

As strange as such preparations seem now, at the time potential attack had to be taken seriously. Long before Japanese troops would actually occupy the Aleutian island of Attu during the Second World War, Lloyd Griscom, U.S. Legatee in Tokyo, warned Secretary of State John Hay about Japanese designs on the island.[10] But even as ominous articles appeared on the front pages of Nome's newspapers, the city's Japanese residents carried on with their lives unmolested. A Japanese cook openly advertised his desire for work; prospective employers could contact him at Nome's Japanese barber shop.[11] And in 1907, when a string of flags was hung across Front Street from Eagle Hall, it included emblems from Europe and Canada, along with the flag of Japan.[12] Nomeites were wary but rarely if ever hysterical. They approved of American empire and martial glory, but they kept their wits about them.

BECOMING ALASKAN

Like many Americans in an imperial age, the Americans on the Seward Peninsula embraced the language of the white man's burden—a phrase Rudyard Kipling brought into English following the outbreak of the Spanish-American War.[13] And, as had been the case since the late 1890s, Nomeites observed that the Eskimo was among the races that were "rapidly disappearing from the face of the earth."[14] For some this was a tragedy, a result of Euro-American depredations; for others it was the harsh if inevitable way of the rough-and-tumble world. Most agreed that the fittest would survive, and the less fit would either have to raise their standards of living—that is, become Westernized—or fall into oblivion.[15]

The concept of fitness that rested at the heart of generic Social Darwinism applied not only to peoples but to nations and towns. The Northland, said one observer, was a place where weaklings could not thrive; it was a place inhabited by the same sort of men who first settled Plymouth Rock and Virginia.[16] But as every schoolchild knew, those settlers had faced great hardship, and Roanoke, England's first North American settlement, had been a failure. Now the Seward Peninsula's early settlers were on the point of learning which of their own plantations would survive and which would not. In 1900 the settlement of York had seemed a place of importance; three years later fewer than ten people lived there. Perhaps as many as four hundred people had lived in Candle City in 1902; by 1904, only a handful remained.[17] By 1906, Dickson, where the Northwestern Commercial Company and a lumber merchant had set up shop in anticipation of a commercial boom, and Solomon, with its six restaurants and five saloons, were dead.[18]

Alaskans knew that survival had partly to do with political status. Nomeites and others on the Seward Peninsula could say, rightly, that their labors had helped to enrich the United States. Partly because of the metal extracted from the Peninsula, and in expectation of what was still to be extracted from it, the U.S. had put itself on the international gold standard.[19] This was real influence.

But Alaskans also believed they had no significant voice in government. They knew that they were unearthing great wealth for the U.S., but the returns seemed meager. This raised the specter of a land pining under the administration of "carpetbaggers" from Outside. "We are in the same position the unhappy South was in after the war and during the reconstruction period," said one writer, revealing, among other things, the extent to which Lost Cause mythology had taken hold far beyond the borders of Dixie.[20] At first, the comparison seems less than apt. Very few who went to Nome came from the South. Among the few who did was William Newton Monroe, who had gone to Nome to supervise the construction of the Wild Goose Railroad, and who, during the war, had fought against the Confederacy.[21] Of another Southerner, a Virginian named John Dexter, we are discreetly told that he "went to Boston after the surrender of Richmond." But even Dexter did not conform to the Southern stereotype: his wife was an Eskimo.[22]

In part, Nomeites' discontent with the federal government was related to skin color. For Southerners of European stock, the preservation of identity meant separating the "races." For settlers on the Seward Peninsula, it meant getting a better deal from Washington than was offered to the dark-skinned residents of the United States' recently acquired islands, especially Puerto Rico and the Philippines.[23] But, so far as Nomeites could see, no such deal was forthcoming. Territorial government, and the greater self-determination that it meant, would not be written into law until August 1912. Until then, Alaskans would wonder at the nice treatment America's dusky islanders received while they, pale and civilized, went all but unnoticed.[24] Alaska would have to take the shape of empire before the dimwits of the world understood its true value.[25]

Lack of territorial status in Washington, D.C., made Nomeites sympathetic to Irish nationalists clamoring for "home rule,"[26] and, as we saw in the previous chapter, it prompted a few to consider annexation to Canada. This perceived absence of political recognition also forced those who remained in the Seward Peninsula beyond the enthusiasm of the gold rush to create and assert an Alaskan identity. Part of this identity involved appreciating, in a grumbling yet good-natured sort of way, the uncommon crosses Nomeites had to bear, such as neighbors' malamutes barking through the night.[27]

As Nomeites brooded, the *Nome Pioneer Press*—not actually a pioneer newspaper (it was first published in October of 1907)—took as its motto "For the interests of Alaska." And Chechacos—that is, newcomers to the Seward Peninsula—received light ribbing from Nome's businesses of the we'll-gladly-take-your-money-too variety.[28] Here, in part, we see an Alaskan identity taking shape: Chechacos were *them*; Alaskans, and especially Nomeites and other peninsularians, were *us*. And now aspiring delegates to Congress were obliged to assert their Alaskanness: H. W. Mellen, running for the nomination of the Democratic Party (he did not get it) reminded voters that he had mined in Alaska for twelve years. Judge C. D. Murane, a Republican who won his party's nomination but not the district's election of 1906, was "an honest and loyal Alaskan, a man loved by all, and an Alaskan of Alaskans."[29] Joseph Chilberg, a Socialist candidate in the election of 1908, was touted as an Alaskan who worked for Alaskans against "Carpetbaggers, Scabherders and the minions of predatory wealth."[30] Frank Waskey, Alaska's first territorial delegate to Congress, had moved to Nome from Minnesota in 1898. That gave him the high status of original pioneer. By 1907 pioneers had high market value. John Feyrer called himself Nome's pioneer tailor, the Northern labeled itself Nome's pioneer saloon, and the Pioneer Candy Company supplied the peninsula's children with Christmastide sweets.

THE FITTEST

In the twentieth century's first decade, Nome's residents could not know what readers one hundred years later would know—that Nome would survive. For them, as for all people at all times, the future was uncertain. Nomeites observed and learned from the experiences of hard-pressed settlements such as Rampart, which was doomed as a trading center. Around the same time that Nomeites learned this, in October of 1906, the *Gold Digger* published a lengthy story on failed towns in Illinois.[31] As they read, Nome's residents kept an anxious eye on their own prospects. Were businesses doing well? Were residents staying in the city through winter? Was the population stable?

By 1910 the struggle for survival among Alaska's gold-rush boomtowns had ended. Skagway had put Dyea out of business, for example, and while Teller, Candle, and Council City would survive on the Seward Peninsula, they would not prosper. This was not what many observers might have expected. Port Clarence, near Teller, had a natural harbor,[32] while Nome's inadequate facilities would not be significantly improved until after 1920—and they would remain inadequate after that. Council was surrounded by spruce trees, useful for building; the Nome region was treeless. Nevertheless, even as early as 1904 all conceded that Nome was the Seward Peninsula's chief city. Three years later it could be said without contradiction that Nome was the peninsula's metropolis.[33]

Before the first decade of the twentieth century had ended, evidence that Nome was the Seward Peninsula's indispensable settlement was easy to come by. Travel through the Seward Peninsula from the Outside usually passed through Nome, and telephone communications on the peninsula were based there. Much of the capital necessary to work elsewhere in the peninsula was raised among Nome's residents, and most of the region's wealth passed through Nome's banks.[34] In the first years of the twentieth century, the Bering Sea district, exclusive of St. Michael and the Yukon River, imported more goods from the U.S. than any other region of Alaska—and most of those goods passed through Nome.[35] Mail to settlements on the peninsula, as well as to the Arctic, first traveled through Nome. Nome's news was the peninsula's news, moreover, and businesses, such as Mrs. Ginivan's Roadhouse in Solomon, were compelled to advertise in Nome's newspapers.[36] Nome served as the peninsula's liquor supply center, and thus was the origin of the alcohol that devastated some of the peninsula's Natives. Along with San Francisco, Nome was where persons who furnished alcohol to Natives were tried and convicted.[37] Nome was central to transportation: stage lines ran from Nome to other points in the peninsula through the winter.[38] And the government agents who gathered in the Seward Peninsula's taxes and sent them to the Department of the Treasury were based in Nome.[39]

In the late summer of 1906 Senator Knute Nelson of Minnesota declared that the Seward Peninsula could eventually become one of three states carved out of Alaska.[40] Given the differences between Alaska's regions, this idea made sense.[41] And were it to happen, there was no doubt that Nome would be the new state's capital. Treasury Department agent Joseph Evans was wrong when he had said a few years before that the Port Clarence region would surpass Nome in importance.[42] By 1907, every previously vaunted settlement on the peninsula besides Nome was in decline.

Nome's greatest challenger to supremacy on the Seward Peninsula was Council, though if pressed Councilites would have acknowledged that most of their business depended, in one way or another, on Nome. Councilites knew that problems between labor and capital in Nome carried implications for residents elsewhere on the peninsula.[43] Monies for the relief of the San Francisco earthquake's victims were collected among Councilites by the Nome Relief Committee.[44] Council's City Meat Market advertised its goods as selling at less than Nome prices.[45] Where Council lacked "veritable miners," Nomeites seemed to make new gold discoveries every day.[46] The Council Aerie of the Fraternal Order of Eagles and the Council Camp of the Arctic Brotherhood provided entertainment for Christmas revelers through 1906,[47] but civic clubs never proliferated there or elsewhere on the peninsula as they did in Nome.

What survives in the historical record tells part of the story. Teller's newspapers, the *Advertiser* and *Musher*, have been lost,[48] and for the period under study here, only some pages of the *Teller News*—in all, about thirteen issues—have survived. The *Candle City News* has also vanished, as has Council's *Totem Truth*. The *Council News* folded in January of 1907. At the time, Nome's two newspapers had the opportunity to regret the loss of Council's last paper: "The suspension of the paper is a sign that the business conditions in Council are somewhat unhealthy."[49]

Frequent typographical errors—"conferense," "Detriot," "Frrnce," "antavonism," "Fairaanks"— bestowed a sense of impermanence on the *Nome Daily Gold Digger* and, in fact, it ceased publication in the summer of 1910. Indeed, in the twentieth century's first decades, most of Nome's newspapers—the *Arctic Appeal, Arctic Brother, Arctic Weekly Sun, Cape Nome Rocker, Nome Mining Gazette,* and *Nome Pioneer Press*—were short-lived. But others—the *Daily Nome Industrial Worker, Nome Daily Nugget,* and *Nome News*—had greater staying power, although all but the *Nugget* would be gone by 1920. After 1907, Nome alone provided printed news for the Seward Peninsula's residents. This was victory.

Almost to Council's end as a boomtown, some of its residents declined to see the obvious. On December 30, 1905, a series of ringing headlines appeared in the *Council City News*:

A PROSPEROUS YEAR

Merchants all Report
Very Lively
Trade

The Holidays Throw A Good
Deal of Life Into
Council

A Glance At the Following Will Con-
Vince the Reader That This is
A Lively Camp

These lines were followed with the sort of forced and fulsome testimonials to Council's economic health that one would expect from businesspeople whose investments were on the point of failure. Mr. Keller, owner of a general store, spoke of the town's business prospects in "glowing terms." The merchants at Irvine, Leslie & Co. claimed to have done their "largest business last Summer." The Marks Hotel said it had confidence in the future. But the greater truth lay in the fact that few businesses were confident enough, or interested enough, in the future of Council to advertise in the local newspaper and, thus, to help it and the town survive.[50] The *Council City News* complained that too few Councilites subscribed to it, though, reputedly, all read it. And the Marks—by 1905 Council's only lodging house—sought to attract customers with free accommodations for twenty horses and dogs.[51]

In the same issue, nevertheless, the *Council City News* acknowledged that pessimists insisted that the town had seen her best days and, with a less than inspiring rallying cry, the newspaper's editor observed, correctly if lifelessly, that "Council has a long life before her but it rests with her own citizens what that life is to be."[52] The trouble was that Council's citizens were leaving, and some of them were resettling in Nome.[53]

The year 1906 was Council's *annus horribilis*. Its newspaper, following the lead of the U.S. postal department, dropped *City* from its masthead. Council City would henceforth be called a town or a camp. In 1905, the *News* had styled itself a "fearless and independent newspaper." By mid-1906 that slogan had also been dropped from the masthead. In the same year several stores had closing sales, and the mail office at Golovin closed. Now mail had to travel to Nome before it could be sorted and returned to Council, adding about a week to the time Councilites would have to wait for their mail.[54] In a time and place where concern over timely access to mail was understandably obsessive, this alone was enough to drive settlers from town.

By 1906 the mines in the Council region had been played out, while the Nome region's wealth remained. The economic depression that had descended on Council was said to be temporary; the town would revive "when we realize the vast unprospected territory tributary to us here." The *Council News* prophesied that the time would come when the town's slacker residents would "look back with wailings and gnashings of teeth to the oversight of opportunities almost within reach." The miners knew better. Among other things, the cost of shipping goods from Nome to Council—as high as $66 a ton—was six to ten times the rate of freight from Seattle to Nome.[55] In its short heyday Council had contributed substantial wealth of the world,[56] but the town's time had passed. The last issue of the *Council News* contained advertisements from the Nome merchants C. D. Dean and C. E. Darling, hardware suppliers, and from J. S. Copley, proprietor of the tavern Board of Trade.[57]

More Councilites moved to Nome where, in any case, most of the business action and civic life had been for several years.[58] By the midfall of 1909 the streets of Council were all but deserted. As the winter of that year descended on the Seward Peninsula, Charles B. Phillips and W. B. Russell, both associated with the Blue Goose Dredging Company, were the last to leave Council for the year. Of course, they would have to meet their steamer to Seattle in Nome.[59]

During summer miners returned to the Council region. In 1912 the enduring Marks Roadhouse (no longer a "hotel") offered "good rooms," "clean beds," and "first class meals."[60] But the chances that Council could again be permanent for more than a few people were small. The same year, N. H. Castle, former editor of the *Council City News*, published a sketch of Council's history. In it, he observed that the settlement had reached its heyday in 1902. He had very little to say of Council beyond that date. He made no attempt to make readers current with events there—partly, one assumes, because there was not much to write about. Castle's own association with Council's main newspaper went unmentioned. And, fittingly, the journal in which Castle's article appeared, the *Alaska Pioneer*, was published in Nome.[61]

Population figures tell a similar story. In 1908, Council was quiet, with a summer habitation of 200. The caption beneath a photograph of Council taken that year referred to it as a "pioneer settlement."[62] Where nearly 700 resided in the Council region in the summer of 1910, that number fell to 109 by 1933. A book published in 1959 with a lot to say about Nome never mentioned Council. In 1971, just 41 people lived there. In the first years of the early twenty-first century, fewer than 10 people resided there year-round. By then, the settlement had not had a post office for over fifty years.[63]

Teller also declined, from a population of about 1,000 in 1910 to 80 by 1920. Nome declined as well from 12,500 in 1900 to 2,600 ten years later. But even in 1920, when Nome's population stood at about 900, it remained the largest settlement on the Seward Peninsula.[64]

For many Nomeites, this was sobering and gratifying. The race to determine which town was fittest had come to an end. Council was no longer a threat. "What in the glorious past was a busy, thriving, populous mining camp will look like a deserted village during the coming Winter," the *Daily Nugget* noted.

> Buildings like the Totem, wherein many scenes of revelry were formerly
> enacted, are now being used as cold storage warehouses, and many structures
> wherein the little ivory ball clicked merrily over the revolving wheel are now
> as silent as the halls of death.[65]

Note the implication that Council had nearly devolved into a Native-like state
of nature. Now it was a "village." The descent into ignominy being irreversible,
the reference to the Totem must have been irresistible: revelry had been swallowed by darkness; exotic ivory had been lost in deathly corridors. The words
were not designed to mean anything precise, save that in the struggle for civic
survival Nome was still standing.

STABILITY

In 1909, when President Taft said that mining camp populations were ephem-
eral, the residents of Nome listened, and they could see that York, Candle,
Davidson, Solomon, Teller, and Council had lost their significance.[66] Relative to
those settlements, Nome was very much alive. Could it remain that way?

Some signs were disheartening. The Northern Commercial Company's
advertisements in Nome's newspapers had brought small returns, and it had
closed its doors in 1903.[67] By the next year, many of Nome's founders—Eric
Lindblom, Jafet Lindeberg, Nels Olson Hultberg, Henry Bratnober, William
Clark, and others—had either left the settlement altogether or fled it in winter-
time.[68] The message seemed to be that those who could afford to get out in the
winter *would* get out. In the minds of people looking for signs of civic vigor,
this was discouraging. Indeed, there was a certain wistfulness among some who
remembered friends and associates who had gone Outside.[69] Getting out of
Nome, even if just for a short while, seemed the thing to do. As if to prove the
point, the Emporium, a men's clothing store in Nome, held a "guessing contest,"
the revealing first prize of which was a ticket to the Outside.[70]

Other omens gathered. By the fall of 1907 the Arctic Brotherhood's baseball
team had lost most of its players to the Outside. At the same time, Nomeites
learned that the Simson Brothers store planned to leave town and needed to sell
everything. The next year, after less than two years in business, the merchant
M. D. Samuels had his own closing-out sale.[71]

Persistent concern about the town's future was manifested in the kind of bold
assertions common in a manly era. "Tho [sic] there may be a certain population

that is not permanent," the *Pioneer Press* declared in August 1908, "the greater portion of the people who are now here will be still calling Alaska their home twenty years from today."

> It is becoming almost habitual for us to say, and to partially believe, that all we desire of this country is a fortune—that gained and we will be off to other scenes. But that is not true. No matter how we prosper we will still make Alaska home and the sooner we realize that we are all here for an indefinite period the better it will be for us and for the country.[72]

The *Pioneer Press's* own indefinite period came to a screeching halt when it went out of existence thirty-one days after delivering this speech. But the faith in the country referred to in the article—a phrase repeated time and again—lived on, and became the stuff of a secular religion whose earthy, dirty, and frequently disappointing deity became more demanding in winter. This creed's ministers commended believers for having "faith in the mineral resources of Alaska," "faith in the mineral resources of this district," and for showing "faith in the future of quartz mining in Seward Peninsula."[73] To be sure, Nome had its churches—in 1904 a Congregational church, an Episcopal church, and a Catholic church—but the sources never give one the impression that traditional piety had much influence in the land of gold, silver, and tin.[74] Faith in the country, whatever that meant, would endure as long as the wealth of the country held out. And that, by itself, lent an air of impermanence to the Nomeites' project. This accounts for what we will see in the next two chapters: the search among Nomeites for something besides mining that could sustain the city.

But in the twentieth century's first decade, the thought that the gold stores might not last forever could be pushed into the back of one's mind, for signs of civic stability could also be seen. Nome was transitioning from a summer camp to a summer *and* winter camp; popular fallacies about Alaska's climate and culture were being met with accurate information; and new buildings were being constructed.[75] The *Gold Digger* observed that there had been steady growth in Alaska's business for several years. "After the first gold rush excitement had abated [Alaska's] trade settled into a natural and healthy condition."[76] Thus, nearly twenty years after the U.S. Census Bureau had declared the American frontier closed, Alaska was serving the role previously played by the American colonies for lower-class Britons and by the American West for young settlers. The vast Alaskan Empire was drawing "hardy, adventuresome workers of the over-crowded communities of the states."[77] In Alaska's great open spaces, boosters proclaimed, millions could get away from the routine and pressures of the American industrial juggernaut that pervaded America's urban centers.[78]

And as the twentieth century's first years passed, Nome became more and more ordinary. City leaders organized a formal Chamber of Commerce and city museum.[79] The federal government established a lifesaving station and Catholic missionaries built Holy Cross Hospital. The U.S. wireless telegraph station at Nome connected the town's residents to the Outside.[80] The Associated Press opened a Nome office in 1909, and civic societies became more active.[81] The Helping Hand Society held dances at the Golden Gate hall, the proceeds from which went to establish a reading library for working men.[82] A baseball diamond, signifying leisure, was built in 1908, and, signifying civility, games were played according to professional rules.[83] The year before, an anonymous donor had paid $10,000 to support Nome's basketball team as it traveled the United States challenging other teams and bringing attention to their hometown. In the early twenty-first century it may be difficult to be interested in forty-minute games ending with scores in the 30s, but Nome's defeat of the University of Kansas (34–28) showed people Outside that Alaskans were as tough as any other variety of American.[84]

Nome shared in the trends of an increasingly corporate age, and companies replaced individual and unorganized miners.[85] Among these were the Wild Goose Mining and Trading Company, the Pioneer Mining Company, the Northern Mining and Trading Company, the Miocene Ditch Company, the Golden Dawn Mining Company, the Campion Mining and Trading Company, the Arctic Mining and Trading Company, the Solomon River Ditch Company, and the Midnight Sun Mining and Ditch Company.

At the same time, freighters, miners, barbers, cooks, and engineers affiliated themselves with the American Federation of Labor and the Western Federation of Miners. Sometimes these local unions brought owners to terms after arriving at compromises. From March of 1906 through late 1908 Nome's progressive Labor Party dominated the city council.[86] The fact that, all the while, Marxism had no chance of taking root in that frozen ground was another indication of the town's place in the politically broad and antiradical American mainstream. And while Nome's lighterage owners had striking workers arrested for agitating against strike breakers, organized labor strife there—as everywhere—grew up amidst a degree of comfort and leisure. The starving and desperate will work for little pay and without complaint, but starvation and desperation were far from Nome's streets.

And government officials continued to recognize the economic potential of the Seward Peninsula. In 1905 the U.S. Geological Survey requested $20,000 to study the mineral resources of the Nome region. This was second only to the amount requested for the study of the Yukon–Tanana region ($21,500), and well above that for southeastern Alaska ($7,200).[87] Among the fruits of the Survey's labors over the next several years were informative and helpful, if uninspiring, books titled *Geology of the Seward Peninsula Tin Deposits* (1908), *The Gold Placers of Parts of the Seward Peninsula* (1908), *Mining in the Seward Peninsula* (c. 1910), *Nome and Grand Central Quadrangles* (1913), *Surface Water Supply of the Seward Peninsula* (1913), and *Lode and Placer Mining on Seward Peninsula* (1917).

Civic stability also meant the acquisition of Edwardian respectability. Accordingly, calls were issued in Nome for the rejection of business applications for new saloons, even if that meant a loss of much-needed municipal revenue. Nomeites were challenged not to litter the streets and neighborhoods.[88] Residents urged the city council and businessmen to legislate Sunday into a day of rest.[89] A Nomeite named Charles Dye was arrested for adultery; his bail was set at $1,000.[90] One historian surmises that, by the end of 1907, Nome had become too quiet for the fiery editor of the *Gold Digger*, J. F. A. Strong, who left the town for more fulfilling ventures.[91] E. S. Harrison's impressive account of Nome's first years (published in 1905) has nothing to say about the romantic miners and fun-loving "good-time girls" late-twentieth-century writers and tourists grinned over. For Harrison, the chaos that accompanied the stampede of 1900 was embarrassing. Instead, readers learned that by 1904 Nome had developed into a stable community, where telephones worked, heated stage coaches to mining fields were available, undesirables were chased out of town, and murderers were hanged.

The efficient justice meted out by Nome's bankruptcy court was yet another indicator of stability. Fred Herd, for example, was a restaurant keeper indebted to the North Pole Bakery, the Snake River Grocery, the Moonlight Water Company, and numerous other businesses. An inventory of his personal property revealed the little he owned—inexpensive cooking utensils including five egg cups, two butter bowls, four meat hooks, and nine cracker dishes. He also confessed to owning "a few broken packages of spaghetti," although he doubted they had any value.[92] Herd, like many others, chose to stay and face his creditors in Nome rather than flee to the Outside as one might have expected a young man to do in Nome's earliest days. Nome was a place where valued early twentieth-century abstractions—progress, order, respectability, honor—could be enjoyed.[93]

If observers wanted further proof that things had settled down, they could have noted that, where there had been eighty-two cases brought to Nome's admiralty court between 1899 and 1903, there were only about half that number in the ten years following. By 1915, boat owners unconcerned about their crews' health, like traders indifferent to the effects of alcohol on Siberia's Natives, were put on notice; the Nome region was still a frontier in only a very limited sense. Law and order, along with a commitment to decency, had taken root alongside Nome's usual preoccupation, the accumulation of wealth.[94]

Indeed, order was established explicitly for the purpose of gaining and protecting wealth. Consider that newspaper editorials decrying the loss of some fifty businesses to fire in September of 1905 were offset by news of a gold strike. Sympathy for the victims of the "Fire God" was balanced with the upbeat observation that a summer never passed through Nome without lead-

FIGURE 10. *"Dinner Party," Lomen Family Collection, acc. no. 72-71-1465, Archives, Alaska and Polar Regions Department, University of Alaska Fairbanks.*

ing its residents to new gold deposits. Solemnity over the burned quarter of the city was displaced by the "greatest activity" that, two days after the conflagration, was motivating men and women to rebuild.[95] This proved that so long as there was substantial wealth in the ground, Nomeites would bend to the will of Providence, the most popular deity in the late-Victorian pantheon. And, indeed, 1906, the year following the great fire (and the year of Council's unraveling), was the Seward Peninsula's richest: gold worth $7.5 million was hauled out of the ground.[96] The following year saw nearly as great a yield.[97] By 1916, over $74 million in gold had been taken from the Seward Peninsula.[98]

The Fire God would visit Nome again in 1934. This time his depredations would be much more devastating if still not fatal. By then, there would be less gold in the Seward Peninsula to comfort and console. Yet many Nomeites stayed past the first great fire, and they continued to create a small society that in many ways was little different from towns Outside.

The city carried on as if it were not unusual at all. There may have been some strict Sabbatarians in Nome in August of 1907, but that did not stop the soldiers at Fort Davis from challenging the Nome Eagles to Sunday baseball games.[99] There may have been some who, innocently if ignorantly, wondered about the usefulness of Latin in the modern world, but, as we shall see, that did not prevent students from taking four years of it at Nome's public school.[100] There was sometimes a feeling that nature was the enemy: was Nome destined to be washed off the face of the earth?[101] But this did not prevent Nomeites from seeing that, sometimes, their city's weather was better than the Outside's. While one blizzard "raged in Kansas, the Nome climate felt sultry."[102]

Life in Nome was difficult. No one denied that. But, as Nome's editorialists never tired of saying, there was much to be grateful for. "Let us laugh with the children and be young," one of them advised a week before the longest night of winter.[103]

> There are two kinds of sunshine in the world, and both quite necessary—the one which is caused by the sun's shining outdoors, and the other by its shining in our hearts. Happy homes abound in the heart of sunshine, and whether it shines without or not, there is naught but brightness within doors.[104]

The triteness of the thought should not overshadow the achievement and endurance it represents.

CHAPTER 4

COMMUNITY

*Embossed in the center of the [city] seal is the figure of a miner with his pan
and shovel, and surrounding him in a circle are the words* Auro sub nive
ditesco—*I acquire wealth from the gold of the beach sands. This is no in*
hoc signo vinces *mot* nor are the golden sands our only source of wealth.
To our minds, all roads lead to Nome as once they did to Rome.

—G. J. Lomen, undated speech[1]

Normalcy, a word the British historian Hugh Brogan calls a "revolting"
American neologism, figured prominently in American public life in the
early 1920s.[2] The election campaign of Warren Harding, who became
president in 1920, called for a "return to normalcy." The experiences of
the decade before had sated the American appetite for rapid change. Enough of
immigration, many Americans thought. Enough of radical left-wingers running
wild in the streets. Enough of American involvement in Europe's problems.
Ideas such as these were broadcast on the radio, which in the 1920s became
the entertainment medium of choice for many Americans. By 1930, Americans
owned some thirteen million radios.[3]

In these things Nome was different. Because Nomeites had an economic
interest in Siberia, they did not share the general American enthusiasm for iso-
lationism. And while Nome's residents had radios, the dearth of references to
them in newspaper commentary and memoirs suggests that they did not take
hold there. The Chamber of Commerce informed outsiders, briefly and almost
as an afterthought, that Nomeites owned radios.[4] But signals from other population centers could not be received in the city during summer, and economic
means were insufficient to sustain a local, self-governing station.

PUBLIC LIFE

The absence of radio entertainment in Nome set the city apart from an important part of the American experience, but it may also partly explain the city's

vibrant public life. There are too many claims in the primary sources of the entire town participating in events not to believe that, for all the transience of the population, the city experienced a high degree of social interaction.[5] In a three-week period, Carl J. Lomen recorded a social life that was probably typical of Nome's ambitious businessmen: two dances, two skating parties, a billiards tournament, a basketball game, a few choir practices, and a trustee meeting at the Pilgrim Church. One suspects he left other events out of his terse daily record.[6] The Lomen brothers' photograph shop was itself a gathering place and destination of visitors to the city.[7]

By 1917, Nome had added an Auto Club and five Masonic orders to an already busy civic life.[8] The Order of the Eastern Star had about 150 members; the Ancient Arabic Order of the Mystic Shrine had about half that number, but it was honored in 1909 and 1912 with visits from the Nobles of the Mystic Shrine on a "pilgrimage" to Nome from the Outside.[9] The first event was memorialized with Esther Birdsall Darling's well-meaning but awful poem "Es Selamu Aleikum."

FIGURE 11. *"Stage/Flag," Lomen Family Collection, acc. no. 72-71-1649, Archives, Alaska and Polar Regions Department, University of Alaska Fairbanks.*

Search, if you will, the tents of Bedouin sheiks—
And meet the Arab in his desert home—
You find no truer welcome than we give,
Nor warmer hearts than beat in Arctic Nome.[10]

The Elks Club received comparable literary notice to the effect that if Kipling were in Nome today "he'd write far finer verse than that on Mandalay." Nome's Irish and Norwegians, too, received tribute.[11]

Through Nome's second decade, the Fourth of July was the city's most public day, the embarrassing lack of celebrations in 1905 serving as a spur to city leaders.[12] Thus each Independence Day crowds gathered to listen to readings of the Declaration of Independence, to watch Fort Davis's soldiers march in parade, and to enjoy bands playing open-air concerts. Throughout these years Nomeites also observed Children's Day[13] and took advantage of performances from the Nome Brass Band. Fort Davis was a year-round center for fun and games;[14] the public-minded Federated Church sponsored bazaars, doll-making contests,

FIGURE 12. *"Children's Day," Elizabeth Wood Collection, acc. no. 2000-101-413,*
Archives, Alaska and Polar Regions Department, University of Alaska Fairbanks.

pageants, and holiday spectacles;[15] and the Eskimo Methodist church held special Easter services to which all were invited.[16] In the municipal elections of
April 1917, nearly 98 percent of eligible voters cast ballots,[17] and during the
campaigns even rival aspiring politicians got along.[18] The word *community* is a
moving target; early twenty-first-century newspaper readers would learn about
something called the "global community." But if the word essentially points to
a social setting where residents participate in public events and promote the
common good, then Nome not only was a community in the most basic sense,
but its inhabitants enjoyed sharing in their common civic enterprise.

Between 1907 and 1917 the business life of the Nome region experienced
ebbs and flows. Fisheries, not gold mines, produced the bulk of Alaska's exports
in these years,[19] but at the end of this period the *Mining and Scientific Press* listed
forty-two dredges on the Seward Peninsula, only ten of which had been built
before 1910.[20] In April of 1917 there was a mini–gold rush to Dime Creek where,
it was thought, large gold deposits were to be found. There was talk of a new
town being built near the new finds; one man said he might build a movie theatre there.[21] In the event, no new town was planted and not much was lost.

In Nome itself, the Alaska Lighterage and Commercial Company began
to sell Dodge automobiles,[22] the Miners Restaurant opened for business, and
Milo's Café closed and then reopened. The M. J. B. Coffee Company promised its customers fresh beverages; the Nome Coffee House and Bakery offered
"wholesome bread"; the Board of Trade offered "family liquor"—that is, non-
alcoholic drinks.[23] In 1916 Nome voted to rid itself of alcohol.

Nome's early reputation as a dashing land of booze stood against the norm
of early Alaskan experience. Alaska had been legally dry before 1889. After
that, high fees were placed on tavern owners and alcohol peddlers to Natives
were prosecuted. Sitka had passed its own prohibition ordinance in 1913 while
Nome's temperance advocates, including its branch of the Women's Christian
Temperance Union, hounded the city's saloons and "boozeologists." Three
years later, two-thirds of Alaskans voted in favor of a prohibition statute, called
the "Alaska Bone Dry Law." Only Chena, Eagle, and St. Michael voted against
the legislation, which went into effect on January 1, 1918.[24] According to the
Nugget, prohibition arrived without fanfare.[25] At that time Nome hosted at least
ten saloons. The Nevada, the Eagle, the Northern, the Angelus, the Board of
Trade, the Golden Gate Bar, and the Nome Brewing Company adjusted to the
dry regime; the Montana, the Headquarters, and the Horseshoe closed their
doors rather than cater to alcohol-free tastes.[26]

Between 1910 and 1920 Nome remained a town more devoted to civil and social religion than to the fervent evangelicalism of much of rural America. The sources are peppered with references to church services and church-supported social events, but they are void of the language of personal religious faith. Carl Lomen recorded church activities in his diary, for example, but he never wrote about his personal beliefs. What little religious language there is in Nome's newspapers during these years is vaguely Christian and forced. In July 1916 Dr. John Parsons preached a "nature sermon" at the Congregational church titled "Men and Trees."[27] And, to cite another example, the *Nugget*'s Christmas editorial of 1917 was replete with dutiful but unfelt clichés that forced its bored author into a syntactical abyss.

> If He of whom it is told that He gave His life for humanity, had left us no other heritage than this one day, His life would have been well lived, for, truly, on that day humanity comes near to godliness and virtue through opening its heart to kindness and charity.[28]

Such inoffensive words could have been accepted by deists, agnostics, Catholics, Methodists, and fundamentalists who, although probably all represented in Nome, never made religious differences a matter of public dispute. Their enthusiasms were expressed in other ways.

DOGS

Among the things that drove Nomeites to untypical fervor, beginning in 1908, were the All-Alaska Sweepstakes dogsled races. The town nearly came to a standstill when the race was on: business slowed and school adjourned.[29] Between 1912 and 1916, the races received pages of coverage in Nome high school's annual publication, the *Aurora*.

From Nome's beginning, dog teams had struggled with cartloads of prospectors' supplies, and settlers had driven them from villages and mining sites into town for shopping. In the winter, when mail from the Outside was coveted, the happiest sound was that of the mail-carrying dogsled team that carried mail to Nome from Kotzebue and from Nome to Unalakleet.[30] When locomotives stopped running on the Seward Peninsula, freight and passengers were pulled along the tracks by "pupmobiles."[31] So the sled races made entertainment of skills forged by necessity. The first race from Nome to Candle—about 440 miles—took place in April of 1908 and was completed in just under five days.

Nome's residents were kept apprised of its progress by a telephone line established on the road between the towns by A. E. Boyd. The winner's purse of 1909 was $2,500.[32]

The races, and the reliance on huskies and malamutes that they represented, added something to Nomeite identity. Nomeites used the races to promote their city. Their advertisements depicted a settlement that was both unusual and ordinary. One promotional booklet included a photograph of the Kennel Club's president, E. E. Hill, a physician, along with advertisements from M. D. Samuels' drycleaners, the Lobby (a pub), Freeding and Borgen's grocery store, and the Nome Bank and Trust Company. The Board of Trade advertised itself as the place to go for insight on who would win the race, "the greatest event in the annals of sport the world over."[33]

Like the gold rush before it, this addition to Nome's civic identity gave birth to a small library of myth-building texts with titles like *Baldy of Nome* (1917), *Seppala: Alaskan Dog Driver* (1930), *Gold, Men and Dogs* (1931), *"Scotty" Allan: King of the Dog-Team Drivers* (1946), and *Wolf Dogs of the North* (1948). Some of these works were more factual than others; all of them were essays in romanticization—food for souls weary of world wars, radical agitators, and economic depression. There are few surprises in them: Here a ferocious dog on the point of being put to sleep is redeemed by a heroic sled driver; there an angelic canine saves its master from frosty death. The following lines capture the genre:

> We saw the night camps on the wind-swept tundra! Where man and dog crawled between canvas-covered toboggans and snuggled together to live. We learned to know his dogs, their peculiarities, their loyalty. They march before us even as we write, those record holders of the wilderness trails! Tuesday!—incomparable leader, veteran of twenty thousand miles! Major, killer dog!—unconquerable spirit of the wilds.... Tip!—brother of Major— his huge bulk one mass of loyalty. Sox! Sunday! Brownie![34]

With temperatures so high, it is easy to see how a person who alleged that a dog was attacking sheep would lose his case in a civil court. "Is there a man among you," a defendant is supposed to have said, "who actually believes that this great trail Malemute *would stoop to attack mere sheep*? All Alaska awaits your verdict."[35] Published in the era of McCarthyism, the Hiss trial, and the advent of Chinese communism, the memoirist's recollection of tundra justice must have tickled the reading public. Thus began the evolution of Nome's public face from that of the miner to that of the hardy sled driver in a small sea of loyal pups.

LEARNING

Another expression of Nome's sense of community was its productive, if unstable, high school. The transience of Nome's population took its toll on the school, which experienced constant turnover among its teachers.[36] The *Aurora* noted in 1914 that "Prof. Karrer has expressed his intention of leaving for the States this year, so this is his last term here"; and "Three more of our schoolmates, James, Eugene, and Jerome, leave . . . this spring."[37] The next year the *Aurora* announced that two more students would soon be leaving the "Little Northern High School, on the frozen tundra drear."[38] In 1930 the school had no graduates; the next year it had four.[39]

This instability translated into few opportunities for students to benefit from long-term relationships with experienced teachers. In 1912 Lucile Wilson taught English, art, and music; F. X. Karrer taught mathematics, science, and German; and S. R. Wilson taught Latin, history, and economics.[40] None of those teachers remained three years later, when Rannie Baker taught English, history, and music while Marion McConaughy taught German, Latin, and gymnastics. In 1916 Baker was still teaching and was joined by Edna O'Connor (German and Latin) and O. W. Baird (mathematics, economics, and science).[41] Continuity and mentoring were difficult to come by.

And yet genuinely good educations were somehow made available to Nome's young people. Although the curriculum would be altered from time to time, partly as a result of concerned parents harassing school administrators and calling for reforms,[42] Latin was at the heart of Nome's secondary studies. The student writer Alfred Lomen appreciated the study of Latin for the way it developed the mind, and there was little resistance in Nome to this focus on a supposedly "dead" language.[43] Nome's young scholars also studied mathematics, French, German, physics, chemistry, history, civics, physical geography, bookkeeping, and physiology.[44] They studied English, and they learned not only to read Chaucerian prose but to reproduce it:

> At Nome there wendes to high scole any day
> Full twenty scolers in a compaignye.
> Hir parkas were adorned with wolverine,
> And alle wrought ful weel with seal skin,
> Hir scole bags and hir pouches every deel.

The poem carries on for thirty-nine more lines.[45]

Many of Nome's students excelled academically, and they went on to colleges and universities at a rate that is impressive even by early twenty-first-century standards. All three of Nome High School's 1908 graduates intended to continue their educations.[46] Of the twenty-three alumni listed in the *Aurora*'s 1914 edition, nearly 50 percent (ten) had gone to, or had already graduated from, a postsecondary educational institution—preponderantly the University of California at Berkeley and the University of Washington. Even more extraordinary, given the norms of the day, was that seven of these ten were women.[47] The *Aurora* could say with justice that Nome High School equipped students for entrance to excellent colleges and universities in the Outside.[48]

Nome's young people accomplished what they did because the subculture they lived in was, generally speaking, well educated and intelligent.[49] Its large number of well-educated professionals—lawyers, doctors, government officials, and military officers[50]—set a tone that promoted thoughtfulness. Irving Reed, who spent his childhood in Nome, inaccurately remembered the city as a place where adults believed that boys of high school age should work and not bother with books. There certainly must have been some who held that view. But Reed himself attended high school in Nome—he was captain of its basketball team—and he went to college in the Outside.[51]

Visitors to Nome sometimes commented on the community's intelligence,[52] and the editors of an early issue of the *Aurora* observed that among Nome's inhabitants were many graduates of leading universities.[53] The appearance of a comet over Nome spurred some to study astronomy; city leaders organized public lectures; and speeches delivered in Nome were often peppered with Latin quotations and references to classical and biblical figures.[54] In 1917 Nome was just one of three Alaskan cities with two newspapers.[55] The level of discourse usually offered by Nome's newspapers points to an educated and perceptive readership.

RHETORIC

There were, of course, instances when the temperance and reflectiveness of the city's public culture were tested. One might expect that during wartime (1914–1918), when censorship was widely accepted, some of the war-related news Nomeites read would be inaccurate or injudicious. In late 1915, for instance, before the carnage of the Somme and before the reported body counts of the war's major battles were known to be factual, the editors of the *Daily Nome Industrial Worker* referred to talk of the war's horrors as humbug and claimed that as many laborers died every year in factories as did in the fields of battle. More striking, though, is the intelligence—along with the increasing ferocity—that characterized most of the *Worker*'s editorials. "Pile on these horrors [of industrialization] in one enormous total," the socialist paper urged,

> the victim of poverty and unemployment and the victim of employment, the number who fill prisons, who are driven to crime and the penalties of crime, the suicide and the prostitute, and compare coldly and reasonably and impartially this war with all its terrific horrors, and it will be doubted that after all is said and done, war hasn't the best of it. It at least feeds, it at least shelters, it at least clothes, it at least justifies. It may be a murderer, but it kills with an open eye and face to face. Peace is the coward, measuring out a lingering death, killing with fearsome and stealthy step from behind, and as from an ambush. It hides its horror and denies it. War admits its iniquity and glories in it.[56]

One need not approve of the central idea expressed here—that, in a gruesome sense, war is superior to capitalism in that it kills openly and unapologetically while smiling capitalists quietly grind laborers—to appreciate that such eloquence was offered to readers in what was supposed to be an American backwater. The *Worker*'s readers were miners, restaurant workers, boat crew members, and barbers.

At the time the *Worker* made this observation, in late 1915, it was becoming more combative and, consequently, pitting itself against Nome's prevalent moderation. The *Worker* had been a socialist journal since it began publication in 1907, but its political commitment was not always obvious, and it is not immediately clear why its tone reached so high a pitch at this time. It was not customary, after all, for its editors to launch harangues against the "militarism" of the Boy Scouts and to denounce capitalism as the "torch bearer of destruction."[57] Most of the time, the paper had to bend to market forces; it relied substantially on advertisements. Indeed, the more intemperate the *Worker* became, the closer it brought itself to its own demise. In place of holiday greetings in December 1918, readers were treated to an article titled "Why I Joined the Socialist Party";[58] in lieu of "Joy to the World" readers got this:

> The smug and sweet content of the world's ruling class is being shaken loose from its normal placidity by the appearance of a cloud upon the horizon that is frought with such sinister and deadly significance as to bring all frightened shivers to the soul of even the most callous and phlegmatic of the ruling and robbing tribe.[59]

Little wonder the paper lost readers. In May 1918 the daily publication became the *Tri-Weekly Nome Industrial Worker*. Six months later it became a weekly. In June of 1919 it went out of business.

LABOR

Moderation does not mean the absence of conflict or argument. But it does point to a commitment to resolving difficulties without resorting to radical means. Thus, even as socialists temporarily gained influence in Nome, the violence that often accompanied their actions in the American states—either as a result of their own actions or as a result of antisocialist reactions—never materialized. Nome's smallness and isolation left its residents with nowhere to go in the event of conflict. They *had* to get along, or at least to tolerate one another. In 1906 the Nome Mine Workers' Union combined with the American Federation of Labor to win the mayoralty and five city council seats on the Labor Party ticket. This marked the peak of the socialists' influence in Nome. Two years later the socialist mayor, Joseph Chilberg, campaigned unsuccessfully to be Alaska's delegate to Congress.[60]

The main reason for the weakness of socialism in Nome was that very few of its residents were opposed to capitalism itself, and fewer were interested in Marxist preaching. Many Nomeites favored progressive ideas—an eight-hour work day and the abolition of child labor,[61] along with the right to unionize and strike. Many also supported women's suffrage. But few were diehard socialists. The Nome Mine Workers' Union president, Philip Corrigan, had to win a seat in the territory's legislature in 1916 by shunning socialist rhetoric, emphasizing instead his experience as an ordinary man of the working class.[62] If the rumor was true that several communist "Nome comrades" had gone to Siberia to join the Soviet revolution of 1917, the adventurers could be assured that very few others would follow them. And if it was true that a handful of Nomeites contemplated linking Alaska to Russia via a "Nome soviet," it was much truer that the great majority of Nomeites would have considered such a scheme outrageous nonsense.[63]

The fact was that Nomeites had little interest in ideological fervor of any kind. The electrically partisan, boring, and short-lived *Nome Democrat* had little influence. Its editor, Hugh O'Neill, cried that under the baleful influence of Alaska's Congressional Republican delegate James Wickersham, Nome was being treated "as a community of Mexican peons or Russian serfs."[64] But while many Nomeites agreed that they were not getting a square deal from the government, they were realistic enough to know that this kind of talk had little basis in fact. Some Nomeites had seen, and most had heard about, what poverty in eastern Russia looked like, and there is no evidence that a single Nomeite ever chose to reside permanently in Russia. But hundreds of Russians had immigrated to Nome, and some had stayed. The message this sent to Nomeites helped to make them immune to the anti-Americanism of the radical left.

At the same time, many Nomeites were also immune to the Republican Party's uncritical acceptance of corporate monopolies. An early target of the Nome press had been the Guggenheim Corporation—"the Guggs"—which sought to corner Alaska's coal, copper, and oil markets, as well as to control much of its railroads. All of the Syndicate's investment, and most of its labor force, came from outside Alaska; its operations were controlled by the corporation's directors; and its partnership with the New York financier J. P. Morgan made it instantly suspect. One historian calls the Syndicate's power in Alaska "colonial capitalism."[65]

For a time the Syndicate rivaled the federal government as a target of Nomeites' anxiety. In 1908 it had bought rich copper mines in the Chitina River Valley in south-central Alaska, and it controlled the Alaska Steamship Company, whose eighteen ships called at Nome as well as other ports. The Guggenheim steamships gave preferential rates to other corporation subsidiaries and the corporation's lobbyists succeeded in obtaining a reduction on taxes on Alaskan fish exports, which led to less money in the territory's coffers.[66] By the time the copper mines in the Chitina Valley were purchased, the Guggs controlled the Northwestern Commercial Company, which had influence on the Seward Peninsula: it owned two general stores (one in Teller, one in Nome), the Wild Goose Railroad, and interests in the North Coast Lighterage Company, which ferried people and goods to and from ships anchored off Nome's coast. It also had stock in Nome's electric company.

Everyone in Nome used electricity (to which the Guggs were linked), Nomeites still hoped for a railroad (which, it seemed, the Guggs might be able to deliver), and the company's merchants and lighterage workers provided basic services. The *Gold Digger* had reason to believe the Syndicate was working to make Nome a company town. But unlike its other possessions elsewhere in Alaska, the Syndicate did not take its holdings in the Seward Peninsula seriously. In 1906 it looked into gaining properties from the Miocene Ditch Company and Pioneer Mining Company but it decided against doing so.[67] The Wild Goose rail line, meanwhile, was soon bankrupt and derelict. In 1908 the Syndicate got rid of all its interests in the Peninsula except for investments in electricity and the lighterage company. Within another four years, the Northwestern Commercial Company wanted out of the Peninsula altogether. After then, the only connection the Syndicate had to Nome came via the Alaska Steamship Company.[68] That the greatest foe of labor in the Seward Peninsula turned out to be something of a phantom probably helps to account for the moderation of political feeling in the Nome region.

The political evenhandedness of Nome's population was expressed in elections and responses to popular social movements. Between 1913 and 1933, Nome's voters sent seventeen Independents, seventeen Republicans (including three Independent Republicans), and eleven Democrats (including one Independent Democrat) to the territorial legislature.[69] And while many Nomeites supported women's suffrage, they also denounced the "hooliganism" of radical suffragette demonstrators in Washington, D.C.[70]

The *Industrial Worker*'s own longevity—from 1907 to 1918—also indicates a high degree of civic tolerance, although once the U.S. had entered the First World War, concern over the socialist paper's agenda grew. At the time the U.S. entered the war in April of 1917, the editor of the *Worker* was Martin Kennelly, an Irishman whose anti-British feeling blended with his socialism. Both as an Irishman and as a man of the far left, it was hard for Kennelly to see why the U.S. should bail England out of its crisis. This angered some Nomeites, and Kennelly's seeming highlighting of German war triumphs in the pages of the *Worker* angered them more. Some thought Kennelly manufactured news out of whole cloth.[71] Empowered and motivated by an antisedition law passed in Alaska during the war, a grand jury in Nome indicted him for sedition, but the juries in two separate trials failed—or refused—to find him guilty. His colleague at the *Industrial Worker*, the even more radical Bruce Rogers, was also put on trial, and he was convicted. Among other inflammatory statements, Rogers had mocked Americans who defined patriotism as a willingness to die "in defense of the trade supremacy of the British Empire and her subjugation of India and Ireland."[72] But this was not the sort of thing to say in a town where, on June 20, 1918, Nome's first twenty-six men selected to serve in the wartime army were admired by gathering crowds.[73]

NATIVES

Given the common racial views of the early twentieth century, one might expect that relationships between Nomeites of European extraction and Alaska Natives would be strained. But even here, Nome's residents proved themselves surprisingly accommodating.[74] It is true that segregationist schemes were put into effect on the Seward Peninsula, during this period, although with little success.[75] It is also true that some Nomeites considered Natives inferior and preferred for them to stay out of town, but this did not prevent Nomeites from being influenced by Natives and from taking an interest in them. Nomeites readily adopted Native words into English— *kayak, cheechaco, husky, malamute, mukluk, parka,* and *umiak*—and they published glossaries of Native expressions, which, at least, suggests anticipated interaction. Some Nomeites studied Native words and phrases they had written in their diaries, and some became fully conversant in Native languages.[76] This latter group included American husbands of Inupiaq women and traders who learned Inupiaq for business purposes.[77] Meanwhile, children were encouraged to learn Native words, and some of them picked up Inupiaq while playing with Native friends; Nomeite parents gave Native items, such as bows and arrows, to their children as gifts.[78] Elizabeth Wood, a fervent photographer of her family's life in Nome, memorialized her son and three Native boys as "four of a kind."[79]

The city's high school students also studied Native terms, and through the first decades of the twentieth century almost every edition of the *Aurora* included thoughtful articles on Natives.[80] In 1910, the *Aurora*'s lead essay was titled "The Eskimo of Alaska."[81] At the commencement ceremony the same year, Helen Kreps read a paper titled "Eskimo Legends."[82] Even eighteen years later, interest at the high school in Native life remained high: the essay "An Eskimo Fish Story" and the poem "The Little Eskimo" won awards.[83] In 1928, one of Nome High School's distinguished graduates, Helen Lomen, published a children's novel about Natives.[84] If Nome's residents thought of the Natives as a "parasitic nuisance," as one historian puts it, they had an unusual way of showing it.[85]

THE COURTS

The theme of this chapter has been the generally peaceful public culture of Nome in the years 1907–1917. This does not mean that Nomeites were immune to the joys of scandal. At the same time that some of Nome's own young men were in harm's way in a European war, the *Nugget* published a call for information on divorces, arrests, embezzlements, and eloping couples.[86] But even this helped to maintain Nome's social structure, for nonconformists and residents lacking personal control knew that they would be held up to ridicule. People who complained about or "knocked" the city were advised to leave it.[87]

Social concord did break down in Nome's courtrooms; the relatively small—yet still ponderous—portion of court documents that survived the fire of 1934 point to a society that, while harmonious in its public life, was also impressively litigious. Sometimes the interests of aggrieved parties and journalists converged, such as when Avanna Langdon divorced William, her abusive and usually absent husband.[88] Julia Smith, another abandoned wife, also divorced her clueless husband, John. An adulterous Myrtle Henderson surrendered her marriage to James without a fight. And Jennie Turner, not yet seventeen years old, had her marriage of sixteen months annulled. Her husband, probably a soldier from Fort Davis, was in prison in San Francisco, and her new male guardian, a "life-long acquaintance and friend," intended to take her to Seattle once the annulment was acquired. One wonders if the honorable court smelled a rat.

In one way or another, though, most of the cases heard in Nome's civil court involved money. The city sued residents who had not paid property taxes, and Charles Brooks sued the Columbia Mining Company for back wages. Silvanie Sansoucy and James Katerinis sued, respectively, A. A. Chagnon and James Andrew for money owed them. Bridget O'Connel sued W. J. Rowe because, she argued unsuccessfully, the horse stable he had built and insufficiently drained—from which "large quantities of excrement, urine and filth penetrated, issued and flowed"—had chased patrons away from her adjacent boardinghouse.

And so on: The Empire Trust Company sued the Fairhaven Water Company. The American Dredge Building and Construction Company sued the American Gold Dredging Company. The American Manganese Steel Company sued the Nome Consolidated Dredging Company. The Miners and Merchants Bank of Alaska sued the Scandia Mining Syndicate. The Miocene Ditch Company sued the Wild Goose Mining and Trading Company. The Dollar Savings and Trust Company sued the Arctic Mining and Trading Company. The Nome Exploration Company sued the Bear Mining and Trading Company. The Pioneer Mining Company sued Johan Tiberg, a thief with a couple of aliases. The eyes glaze, but these are just a handful of the cases heard in Nome's civil court between 1910 and 1920.

At first the paradox presents a challenge: Nomeites got along and, together, forged a markedly tolerant public life; and yet they sued one another without compunction. But, while the paradox stands, the challenge can be answered with the observation that, in doing this, Nomeites were once again revealing their Americanness. As the millions of immigrants who came to the U.S. before the 1920s could say, America was a far from perfect country, but the migration traffic itself proved that few other nations were as open and accommodating. Yet, at the same time, no country could match the American passion for litigation. In 1900 the U.S. claimed one hundred thousand "ambitious [and] pushy" lawyers—or about one lawyer for every seventy-six residents.[89] The task at hand is not to explain this peculiarity in the American experience, but only to point to it in Nome as further evidence that its residents had succeeded in building an American town that, yes, was unusual in many ways, but was more ordinary than not.

CHAPTER 5

STRUGGLE

We have in Nome many kinds of pro's and con's, but the most active and vir-ulent kind is the anti-Nomeites who are always ready to say and do almost anything to injure Nome's best interests. My advice to the anti-Nomeites is the same as that given by President Wilson to the pro-Germans: "If you don't like the place that you make a living in, why don't you move."

—Polet Stores advertisement, August 1918

WARTIME

In the months before America's entry into the Great War, conflict seemed inevitable, but it was not clear whether the U.S. would fight against Germany in Europe or against Mexico, whose troubled border with the U.S. had been an irritation for years. As in many places in the U.S., attitudes in Nome about the war before America's entry into it were shaped by the indifference or mild curiosity afforded by distance. The 1915 edition of Nome's high school annual, the *Aurora*, provided a "prophecy" of war between the U.S. and Mexico: "The U.S. finally decided to invade Mexico and bring about peace."[1] The following year, the annual made no reference to war. The *Nugget*, meanwhile, hoped that war would not come lest progress on the harbor at the mouth of the Snake River be put on hold. "However, the chances are greatly against our making war," the paper assured its readers, "and the chances favor the appropriation of money for the . . . harbor."[2]

But war came on April 6, 1917, and the town felt the pull of martial enthusiasm. On that day the *Nugget* affixed a prominent American flag to its editorial page, a response to the mayor's appeal for the national symbol to be displayed throughout the town.[3] In early May a patriotic demonstration convened in Nome. One speaker related British propaganda: he told the audience about Germans mutilating and torturing war prisoners and about the Huns' passion for gouging out eyes and crucifying the blameless on barn doors. Dan Crowley,

Nome's "poet laureate," recited a work titled "U. S. (us) for You." Sergeant Chrisman of Fort Davis directed soldiers in marching maneuvers. And Nomeites purchased nearly $42,000 in liberty bonds. Harry Pigeon bought $1,500 in bonds, A. N. Kittilsen $3,000, and Al Gawne $5,000.[4] Most bond purchases were in the $50 to $100 range, still heavy sums at a time when the Nome Miners Union was agitating for daily compensation (wages plus board) that came to about $7 a day.[5] The Arctic Bakery and Candy Store enticed patrons with the possibility of winning a $100 liberty bond in exchange for a 25-cent meal.[6]

Nome's financial contribution to the war effort was praised by officials in San Francisco, who bestowed an "honor flag" on the city.[7] Meanwhile, under the direction of Carl J. Lomen, the divisional food administrator, meal ingredients were altered. One-third of the wheat that formerly went into cakes, pies, and pastries now had to be substituted.[8] The Nome Bakery called the result "Victory Bread."[9]

Nomeites planted improbable "Liberty gardens" with radishes, turnips, and lettuce,[10] and the Nome Loyal Legion passed resolutions calling for the defeat of Germany and for the abolition of dissent, including that of pacifists, whose rhetoric could only help the Germans.[11] Citizens and subjects of Germany living in Nome had to register at the post office between April 29 and May 4, 1918.[12] And, while the *Nome Nugget* indulged in the anti-German speechifying that quickly became commonplace in the U.S., Nomeites of German stock did not experience hardship in their day-to-day affairs. This was another indication of the city's temperance.

Early on in the war effort, Governor J. F. A. Strong appealed for a militia to be created in Nome. The Home Guard that formed drilled for an hour on Monday, Wednesday, and Friday mornings.[13] The Coast Guard cutter *Bear* stood off Nome's coast ready, if needed, to lend assistance to steamers and also, perhaps, to provide rudimentary defense in case of trouble.[14] But Japan, the potential menace long pointed to by Nome's newspapers, was now a nominal ally of the U.S., and by April of 1918, nearby Russia was out of the war. Germany's Asian colonies had been neutralized and posed no threat to the American west coast, let alone to distant Nome. Save for the very slim risk of sabotage of communication lines, which themselves were not important to war aims, the Germans, Austrians, and Bulgarians posed no threat to Alaska. Thus, other than sentries guarding Nome's wireless telegraph station,[15] there was little for the soldiers at Fort Davis, and nothing for a civilian militia, to do.

But Nome did make a contribution to America's war endeavor. Two French

Nomeites went to the conflict early. One of these, René Haas, invited the famous dog racer "Scotty" Allan to gather a team of one hundred dogs to sledge supplies for French troops in the Vosges Mountains. The Nome dogs brought supplies and communication lines to French soldiers cut off by Germans, and before long the war came home in a deeper way: in the midsummer of 1917, about ninety were counted eligible for the draft. Of the nearly thirty Nomeites who were inducted into the military, at least five died—Dahlberg, De Ronne, Olson, Weber, and Geiger—all from influenza or pneumonia.[16] No soldier from Nome died overseas.[17] The Spanish flu epidemic that killed these men in the States came to Nome in the fall of 1918, when 90 percent of Nomeites fell ill and 30 in the town died. Of the 250 Eskimos in the immediate Nome region, just 50 survived.[18]

Day by day the effects of the First World War on Nome did not seem great. But there was a strong sense of foreboding among its residents, especially when they reasoned that supplies the town relied on would fall into short supply. Just before war was declared the Seattle-based Alaska Lighterage and Commercial

FIGURE 13. *"Soldiers March," Lomen Family Collection, acc. no. 72-71-1647,*
Archives, Alaska and Polar Regions Department, University of Alaska Fairbanks.

Company warned Nome's residents that coal would become very expensive, for ships involved in the trade were expected to be commandeered for the war effort.[19] Before long, trading vessels *were* employed for the war. The *Seward*, formerly owned by the Alaska Steamship Company, was torpedoed in the Mediterranean. As if to indicate a desire among the townspeople to have a part in the conflict, the *Nugget* titled its article "Nome Boat Sunk by Submarine."[20]

The Great War also placed demands on materials relevant to the Nome region's mining industry, steel alloys in particular. This led to a decline in mine production. A demand for labor and the higher wages available Outside, meanwhile, created an exodus of young men from the territory.[21] Some of Nome's workers went to shipyards in the States; others may have been lured to the fishing fields of California by enthusiastic news from former Nomeite John Kullish.[22] And while a scarcity of labor in Anchorage led to the employment of "Hindus" as menial laborers, no such foreign workers were needed in Nome. Meanwhile, the *Industrial Worker* doubted that Natives could be convinced to provide rich gold to employers in exchange for "bare subsistence."[23]

In 1918 only half as many men were working on Alaska's railroads as had been the year before,[24] and a strike among laborers in Nome did nothing to improve the local employment scene.[25] The early loss of twenty-six consumers (Nome's military inductees), among them two of the city's most capable young businessmen, Ralph and Alfred Lomen, also hurt Nome's economy.[26] Even the perennially challenging weather seemed worse. "A record season for lateness," Carl Lomen wrote in his diary as he looked in June for trading vessels to arrive at the city. "Ice extends far to the South. The *Vic[toria]* in ice the 9th, and by the 15th is off Nome some thirty miles—The 18th weather brightens, but apparently no change in ice condition."[27] Shops closed their doors.

Writing six years after the war, one of Alaska's early historians surmised that this "drain" of Alaska's "young pioneers," along with the opening of the Panama Canal in August of 1914 and the consequent shift of maritime focus southward, contributed to a decline in investment in the territory.[28]

On the heels of war's end came more bad news—the closure of Fort Davis. Absent the possibility of combat, the soldiers at the fort had little to do during the war, and the fort's troops carried on much as they had before—attending church, maintaining their barracks and uniforms, patronizing restaurants, and occasionally getting into trouble and being periodically banned from saloons.[29] High-ranking officers had recommended closing Fort Davis in 1905 and again in 1908. Presumably, it was not closed at that time because of potential threats

from Asia, or because the Siberian trade might grow dramatically.[30] Or perhaps there would be another gold rush in the Nome region. By August 1919,
though, no serious eastern threat had materialized and the fort's main reason for
being—to prevent disorder in the streets of Nome—had ceased to be a concern,
partly because of the town's orderliness, partly because of war's own effect on
the city. Corporate mining operations now commanded the gold industry and
the prospective wealth of the land was by then well known, thanks largely to the
work of the U.S. Geological Survey. The chances of another rush to the settlement were nil, and the federal government was eager to cut national expenses.
It did not need to pay for the upkeep of troops sequestered in a barely accessible
and unnecessary station.

At full strength, about 135 soldiers served at Fort Davis.[31] One cannot imag-
ine that many of the soldiers stationed there when the fort closed were disappointed. The fort had been a social center almost out of necessity—without
this, the tedium would have led to trouble. In saying very little, the single sentence that appears at the end of every monthly report written between January
1908 and December 1915, under the heading "Record of Events," says a lot:
"The troops of this command performed the usual garrison duties during this
month." Sometimes the drilling, cleaning, shoe shining, and night watching
were supplemented by target practice. Beginning in 1916, the record of events
space in the reports was left blank.[32]

The effects of the fort's closure on Nome's economy were significant, representing the estimated loss to the local economy of about $5,000 a year. The fort's
closing also meant a shrinking of the marriage market for young women on the
Seward Peninsula.[33] Certainly it meant the narrowing of entertainment opportunities. As before, when the possibility of the fort's closure was announced,
Nome's mayor and Chamber of Commerce protested.[34] The soldiers based at
Fort Davis were moved to the fort at St. Michael.

SIBERIA

As Nome's economy slowed during the First World War, Nomeites turned—or,
more accurately, returned—their attention to Siberia.[35] After the war, Nome's
capacity to dictate its own future was weak. If its future were to brighten, then
its economy would have to be linked to another entity or to a different kind
of commerce in which Nome might have a comparative advantage, although
even in the case of the Siberian trade outsiders in the form of Seattle merchants

were a threat.[36] The potential wealth to be gained from Siberia was impressive. According to the *Nugget*, nearly $2 million worth of goods had passed through Nome from Siberia between 1904 and 1918. In the same period, about $600,000 of goods were exported from Nome to Siberia and the Herschel Islands.[37]

But the international scene, over which Nome's traders had no control, was confused, dangerous, replete with mixed messages, and should be briefly described here. Before the U.S. had entered the war against Germany in April of 1917, President Woodrow Wilson had wondered how he could claim, as he did, that the war was about the expansion of democracy when an ally was governed by an autocratic czar. When revolution overthrew Russia's autocracy in March, proclaiming liberal ideals, Wilson's scruples were satisfied. But this new government was soon overruled by communist revolution. Once again, the U.S. faced an autocratic regime in Russia led by Vladimir Lenin.

FIGURE 14. *"Guitar Player," Lomen Family Collection, acc. no. 72-71-1409,*
Archives, Alaska and Polar Regions Department, University of Alaska Fairbanks.

Because the communist, or Bolshevik, government did not control the entire country in its first years, because it had not been elected by a majority of Russian voters, because it refused to pay Russia's debts to creditor nations, and because it disseminated revolutionary propaganda in other countries, the U.S. government refused to recognize the Bolshevik regime, and observers bemoaned the devastation wrought by the "wolves of Bolshevism."[38] As civil war broke out in Russia, the U.S. assisted the anti-communists militarily, albeit in a way that lent Lenin great propaganda material without substantially assisting the anti-Bolshevik cause.

In July of 1918 Wilson gave the order for 5,700 troops to go to Archangel and Murmansk in northern Russia and another 8,000 soldiers to go to Siberia. Among Wilson's concerns were military stores at Vladivostok, Siberia, owned by the anti-German allies, which he feared might come under Bolshevik control. He was also concerned that the Japanese might take advantage of Russia's unsettled condition and take possession of Siberian territory or take advantage of economic opportunities at the expense of American traders.[39] (In the background here was Japan's military victory over Russia thirteen years earlier.) Better to send troops to Siberia in conjunction with the Japanese than to let them go in alone.

Before long, the role of the troops in Siberia was to support the anti-Bolshevik Admiral Alexander Kolchak. After Kolchak was captured and executed in January of 1920, writes one historian, the American presence seemed pointless, and the troops left Siberia in August.

If concern over Nome's small-time trade in Siberia—as opposed to hopes for substantial trade carried on by large American businesses—was a concern to the federal government, it was not a major concern. The U.S. government refused to recognize the Soviet regime in Russia, and a visitor from the Smithsonian Institution to Nome in 1926 had to contact Russia's consul in Montreal to obtain permission to visit the Russian-owned island Big Diomede.[40] U.S. nonrecognition of the Soviet government continued until 1933, even as Congress appropriated $20 million to provide Russia's destitute with food and medical supplies. The Soviets were cooperative in dispersing the aid while simultaneously refusing to acknowledge that it existed.[41]

This was the unsettled and confusing environment Nome's traders faced as they set sail for Siberia. Such was the troubled world Russians left behind them when they left Siberia for Nome, either as traders, immigrants, or escaped political prisoners. For a time the American presence—which is largely to say

Nome's presence—in eastern Siberia seemed more consequential than the Russian government's. Through 1919, the *Nugget* announced at the top of its front page that Nome was America's distributing center to both northern Alaska and Siberia. In the same year, Nome's Chamber of Commerce urged the Corps of Engineers to expedite building a harbor at the mouth of the Snake River, for the city's "mosquito fleet" and its trade along the Siberian coast was growing.[42]

The available evidence the historian relies on to gain an understanding of Nome's exchanges with Siberia is fragmentary. But taken together, the fragments form a picture of an intricate relationship. Most transactions in Siberia were peaceful (the Lomen brothers took many photographs of Natives there);[43] but some were deadly. When, during the First World War, Siberians began to be conscripted into the Russian army, Nomeites read about it, and this brought the war a little closer to home.[44] After 1917, the Russian Revolution and ensuing civil war fundamentally altered circumstances. News of Americans in Russia being attacked by Bolsheviks shaped how Alaskans viewed the new Soviet regime[45] and, in time, caused Nomeites to believe their city was vulnerable to attack, either from rogues posing as Bolsheviks or from actual Soviet agents.

For a span of years preceding and immediately following the Great War and Russian Revolution, Nomeites plied the Bering Sea in boats named *Belinda*, *Nugget*, *Trader*, *Polar Bear*, *Belvedere*, *Augusta*, and *Teddy Bear*, among many others.[46] The Siberia trade may have been helped along by Russian immigrants who came to Nome—about three hundred in 1909 aboard the ship *Varg*, but in steady trickles until 1923, when the Soviets were taking firm control of Siberia.[47] In 1925 an inspector with the Department of Commerce noted in a letter that Russians were in the town—some of them, presumably, refugees, some of them immigrants from earlier years.[48] Russians in Nome were willing to work longer hours than Americans for less pay, and for that reason they were objects of union animosity.[49] Some of those who did not move Outside may have found employment assisting nonunionized American traders as translators in Siberia, especially after a Soviet law required a Russian speaker on every trading vessel.[50]

Early in Nome's history the Siberian trade was fueled by schemes that linked Siberia with Alaska via a railroad or tunnel—a potential boon for Americans, and threat to some Russian officials who worried about an influx into Siberia of American settlers "who would then colonize and then annex eastern Siberia."[51] As the years went by, other interests increased the links between Siberia and the Seward Peninsula. In 1902, fifty miners from Nome went to Siberia with the North Eastern Siberian Company to search for gold;[52] Siberians wanted American clothing and illicit alcohol; and Nomeites wanted Siberian seal-oil lamps, ivory, whalebones, and primitive tools to sell as novelties. Siberian polar bear skins could fetch $200.[53] One shipment of fur that arrived in Nome in 1909 was worth $25,000. Two years later, $200,000 worth of furs and ivory landed in Nome. The transactions of 1911 marked the peak of the Seward Peninsula–Siberia economy, but $115,000 in trade was carried on over the following two years.

Throughout these years, Americans in Siberia were supplied by merchants and traders in Nome, and their mail came to them in Siberia via Nome. In September 1910, the Russian patrol boat *Shieka* anchored off Nome's beaches. The "bright Russian uniforms" of its officers were conspicuous in Nome's streets.[54] But what they were doing there, and what was accomplished by their visit, we do not know. During the First World War, one visitor wrote that Siberian traders could be seen in Nome "at most any time."[55]

Such is the spotty record. Nome's Literary Society heard a lecture on eastern Siberia, but we do not know its substance. A Frenchman is said to have traveled to San Francisco from France via Siberia and Nome, but this appears to have no greater importance than the aura of romance it bestowed on the region. Secondhand accounts claim that Russian political prisoners escaped to Nome. Who these people were and what they did once they arrived, if they really did arrive, are mysteries.[56] The governor of Siberia visited Nome at least once to discuss mining and trade, but it is not clear that anything substantial came from the talks. This was partly because American shippers habitually ignored Russian trading laws and taxes and, most of the time, the pre-Bolshevik government left them alone.[57]

On occasion the Russians tried to crack down. In July of 1916 Nome's Chamber of Commerce sought government assistance against the seizure of American trading vessels by Russian ships,[58] while peddlers of alcohol to Siberia's Natives enjoyed less toleration from either side of the sea. One booze trader, Mike Gottschalk, was sentenced to five years in a Russian prison.[59] At the same time, corrupt Russian officials sought to gain from American labor, in one case taking $10,000 worth of gold prospected in Siberia without paying for it as they had agreed to do earlier. Jafet Lindeberg, director of the mining project and owner of the Pioneer Mining Company, was forced to trek to distant Moscow to receive his due.[60]

A much more apparent direct threat to Nome than the war in Western Europe was the civil war in Russia and the possibility of Russian reprisals against the U.S. for its assistance to anti-Bolshevik forces. Nomeites had heard firsthand about the civil war from anti-Bolshevik Russians who visited Nome and traded there. In September of 1919 Carl Lomen wrote in his diary, with his customary terseness, that sailors from the Russian gunboat *Yakut* were unable to exchange their currency in Nome's banks, although Yankee traders accepted their money at a ratio of twenty-five or thirty rubles to one dollar.[61] These Russians told Nomeites about the war, and this is, perhaps, what Nome's mayor Edgar Holt and Alaska's governor had in mind when they suggested that Fort Davis should stay open while events in Russia remained unsettled.[62]

Their anxiety seemed justified. During the civil war American traders supplied anti-Bolshevik fighters in Siberia and, thus, injected themselves into the conflict. Some of them were detained or imprisoned by the Bolsheviks;[63] others were arrested simply for setting foot on Russian territory;[64] still others were rescued from Russian captivity by Chinese laborers.[65] Later reports told how the Soviet ship *Red October* spirited an American and a few Eskimos from Wrangel Island to Vladivostok, where the American died. The three Eskimos were later sent to northern China, where a British vice consul negotiated the release of the one survivor. The moral of the story for the Seward Peninsula's Alaskans was that someday the Soviets might "sail right into Nome and make off with whatever they happened to want."[66]

This possibility seemed to become reality in the summer of 1920, when L. M. Quirk of Juneau and Corbett Bland of Nome arrived in the city with the story of a battle between Bolsheviks and Alaskan miners that had led to the death of a dozen Russian aggressors.[67] The Bolsheviks had sought to shut down all trade with foreigners, and

> [a] mere handful of American miners, mostly Alaskans, fearful their supplies would be seized, rallied the people to organization, resulting in a good old time western massacre. Mikoff, the leader of the Bolsheviks, was first riddled with .30-30 bullets from the rifles of the armed Alaskans, followed by the killing of many of the Bolsheviks.[68]

The account smells of embellishment, but there is evidence for similar massacres in Siberia,[69] and the effect of such news on the people of Nome was considerable. The *Nugget* took the traders' story at face value, perhaps because there was good evidence of its truth, perhaps because the vulnerability Nomeites felt after Fort Davis closed made believing the story easy. The paper, speaking for many in Nome who had lost business as a result of the fort's closure, also had a vested interest in the account being true. If Soviet predators were only two days' distance from the city, it would be "a very easy matter for an armed band of these desperate characters to cross [the] Bering Sea and transfer their depredations to this coast."

> [W]e are very much lacking [in armed forces] since the government saw fit to abandon Ft. Davis and remove the troops to St. Michael, where they are about as useless for defensive purposes in case of an attack by raiders on Nome as a body of troops in the Philippines. . . . Nome is fully justified in again raising a strident voice for troop protection, even though there is small hope that it will be heard in Washington.[70]

As months passed, Nomeites continued to be apprehensive of Soviet invasion. Beginning in 1923, with the exception of one American store, the Soviets shut down at the gun's point all noncommunist activity. Illicit American traders were completely chased out of Siberia by 1925.[71] Americans were still allowed to carry out search-and-rescue operations—Soviet and American pilots worked together in this way[72]—and under that guise some illicit Yankee trade was carried on. But this amounted to very little, and it was always dangerous.[73] "A few evenings ago the local population was aroused to the realization that two strange craft were approaching from the Siberia direction," a visitor to Nome wrote in a letter to a loved one on the Outside. "Some suggested Bolsheviks coming over to clean house." As usual, it turned out to be nothing special. But the knowledge that the Coast Guard cutter *Bear* was due back from Siberia soon was of some comfort.[74]

For all its exotic qualities, mystery, and appeal, for all the hopes placed in it by some in Nome's business community, Nome's trade with Siberia did not have a great economic effect on the city. Neither would the opening of Siberia to some flights from the U.S. in 1929.[75] Beyond memoirs by arctic traders, passing references in letters and diaries, and books and newspaper reports about them and their exploits, there is little in the sources to suggest that the trade actually touched many Nomeites' lives in an important way. A few of Nome's miners worked Siberia's prospective gold fields,[76] the Siberia trade employed sailors who worked with the ships based at Nome, and it gave periodic work to Nome's lighterage workers, although sometimes this business was done by Natives.[77] Schooner operators also hired Natives who, presumably, would work for less pay than Nome's residents.[78]

Warehouses for the Siberian trade were maintained in Nome, but these would not employ more than a few men.[79] Siberian goods sold in Nome, and timber purchased in Nome by traders for use in Siberia, also brought business to merchants and must have helped to bolster a sense among the people of the city that they were Americans of a different kind.[80] But this did not put significant wealth into many Nomeites' bank accounts or food on many families' tables. Sometimes, because of high surf, schooner crews who worked the Siberian trade did not even come ashore in Nome to buy a meal. Some traders purchased their supplies in San Francisco.[81]

Memoirs of those involved in the Siberian trade themselves actually provide little information about Nome, not because Nome was not important to them but because it seemed so ordinary relative to what they experienced in Siberia. From them we learn about the hope some had of finding the equivalent of Nome's gold across the Bering Sea, and this motivated traders and miners in search of a "Siberian Klondike." From them we read that Nome served as a geographical reference point for sailors from the Outside interested in going to Siberia. We learn that Americans in Siberia sometimes had to return to Nome to send telegrams to the Outside; that American traders buried loved ones and associates in the city; that Nome was a safe haven for sailors caught in arctic storms and the place from which rescue operations for traders in distress were launched.[82] This suggests a lot of movement in and out of Nome, but very little tarrying, and very little money spending. The relevant portion of the *Nugget's* slogan of 1919—"Nome is the Distributing Center and Gateway to . . . Siberia"—was exactly right, albeit not in the way the paper's editor hoped. Nome was a gateway, something for traders and adventurers to pass through, and little more. In the early 1930s Nome was still spoken of as the gateway to Siberia, although by that time the claim hardly meant anything.[83] The Siberian trade had helped to stabilize Nome in that it provided Nomeites with trade and a potentially great future. But since the trade attracted men with adventurous streaks, it also contributed to the environment of transience that had always existed in the city.

Before the U.S. entered the First World War, the *Nugget* observed that it had already taught thinking people that nations "are so dependent upon one another, so inextricably bound to one another with unseen, though none the less indissoluable [sic] bonds, that great national developments in the one cannot but, in some degree, affect the others."[84] In the end, the Siberian trade proved to be both seeable and soluble. Nomeites watched as it, and the ambitions linked to it in their minds, vanished. In this case, the actions of Joseph Stalin had a greater actual and psychological effect on Nome than those of the U.S. government.

The looked-for thaw in U.S.–Soviet relations that would once again spark Nome's economy came briefly during the Second World War when Nome provided Soviet pilots with a fueling stop on the Lend–Lease route from the U.S. to Russia.[85] That war ended in 1945; so did the thaw. References to the Siberian trade do not appear in many of the Alaskan memoirs written for mass consumption through the mid-1940s.

The effects of the Great War, the flu of 1918, the closing of Fort Davis, and the repercussions of the Russian Revolution made Nome a less attractive place to live, although it remained a nice place to visit. "If we were to live in Alaska," a tourist wrote in a travel book published in 1918, "Nome would be our home and her people our people."[86] But by the time of the book's publication, many of Nome's people were leaving. The *Victoria* sailed from there in October with 700 aboard. Between 500 and 600 remained in town to face the winter. The census of 1920 placed the city's population at 852.

CHAPTER 6

SETTLING

Further work [on Nome's harbor] appears justified, but the justification is
to be found in the peculiar situation of the town as a distant and isolated
outpost of the United States, rather than in the analysis of probable sav-
ings. As an outpost, Nome is entitled to special treatment.

—Corps of Engineers, North Pacific Division, 1930

Nome... is a very livable place. It is still a new country, and to live in it
requires a certain amount of pioneer and frontier spirit. Our people have
their joys and sorrows, but the world is made up of both.

—Northwestern Alaska Chamber of Commerce, 1932

I n August of 1923 Nome showed its respects to the memory of President
Warren Harding, who had died soon after a visit to Alaska. Mayor George
Maynard directed all businesses to close their doors on Friday the tenth.
The town's church bells chimed for two minutes, beginning at 10:00 A.M.,
during which time the town's residents stood in respectful silence.[1] Even in an
era when it was acknowledged, as the new President Calvin Coolidge put it, that
the business of America was business, Nomeites recognized that some things
were more important than business—at least for a few moments.

Historian Terrence Cole calls the 1920s and 1930s Nome's "hardest years."[2]
Certainly, these years unveiled challenges and disappointments. In 1934 the town
came closer to elimination than it had done before or would do after. But the certain hard-headedness that led in the first place to the establishment of Nome on a
harborless, unprotected spot on the Bering Sea coast would continue to prevail.

Yes, these years were difficult. The observations and recollections of passers-
through depict a town on its last legs, as all but evacuated. "The city of Nome is a
town of shreds and patches," wrote one traveler, "the raggedest [sic] municipal-
ity I have yet struck in Alaska. There are houses enough for ten thousand people,

though the population is to-day not one tenth of that."[3] The Golden Gate Hotel in particular came under criticism, perhaps because it was the biggest target in town, but also because, by all accounts, it was run-down and expensive. Merely pressing a button to call the bellboy cost ten cents,[4] and its rooms smelled of "old sweat, old blankets, and mold."[5]

But all the news was not bad. The 1920s saw a near doubling of the population from the low recorded by the census of 1920. When the great fire of 1934 broke out, between 1,200 and 1,500 people lived in Nome. And in 1925, one potentially devastating disaster—an outbreak of diphtheria—was mitigated, or seemed to be, by the Alaskan pluck and dash outsiders had come to expect. In the depths of winter, antitoxin was rushed to Nome from Nenana by a series of dogsled drivers. Whether, in the event, the antitoxin was actually needed as much as some believed is less interesting than the feat itself, which made national news and led to the planting of a monument of the run's best-known dog, Balto, in New York's Central Park. The far north was further romanticized. Neither of the two books that chronicle these events could avoid the word "heroic" in their titles.[6]

Throughout these years, too, Nomeites continued to look for a route to global significance. Now attention turned to the skies, particularly after August 23, 1920, when four aircraft landed at the defunct Fort Davis.[7] "The City of Nome, already an entrepot for the Far-North Commerce," G. J. Lomen said in a high school commencement address, "promises to become the gateway to an air service, which . . . is destined to fulfill the dream of centuries."[8] In 1928, his sons, Alfred and Ralph, were instrumental in bringing winter passenger service to Nome in the form of Wien Alaska Airways.[9] Indeed, the Lomens seemed more influential than ever. In addition to their businesses, they entertained visitors, organized lectures, and donated Native artifacts to the Smithsonian.[10]

As before, the federal government maintained a presence in the town. In the mid-1920s the government employed at least forty-two residents, including seven Coast Guardsmen, a collector of customs, a judge and his secretary, nine law enforcement officials, three employees with the Road Commission, four with the Signal Corps, and one with the Game Commission.[11] By the early 1930s, the Coast Guard had a permanent shore station in Nome and the Department of Agriculture and Office of Indian Affairs posted agents there.[12] It may be that this presence lacked vigor: "[S]top at the Coast Guard building—no one there; at the Roads Commission—office empty; at the Customs—not a soul."[13] But when emergencies came, employees tended to their duties.

By 1930 the value of the Seward Peninsula to the U.S. was clear. In no year between 1923 and 1929, by which time gold production had fallen off substantially, was less than $1 million in gold shipped from the peninsula to the Outside. In 1931 the thirteen dredges operating in Nome produced over $1.3 million in gold.[14] Nome's value also lay in its status as the center of organization on the peninsula. And, being some five hundred miles west of Hawai'i, it was the U.S.'s northwesternmost possession. "Nome is the center of the economic life of a very extensive region embracing the coastal portions of western and northern Alaska, northeastern Siberia and Kamchatka, and the Islands of the Bering Sea," a government report noted. "It is the only white settlement of any consequence in this entire region and is the center of American influence there."[15]

Nome's symbolic value could not be quantified but neither could it be minimized. As an economic entity, Nome could hardly compete with San Francisco or Seattle, but on the Seward Peninsula it was unrivaled. In 1925 over $1 million in goods was shipped to Nome and the same amount in gold was exported from there.[16] At this time the United States Smelting, Refining and Mining Company, known locally as Hammon Consolidated, dominated the gold fields, and it remained in Nome until 1962.[17]

ROADS AND THE HARBOR

As Nome's economy and population waxed and waned in the 1920s and early '30s, the government spent money on the region's infrastructure. In the spring of 1917 Nome's Chamber of Commerce and Automobile Club and Miners' Union had lobbied the territorial legislature to pass a roads appropriations bill.[18] In the summer of that year the Alaska Road Commission had made a road from Council to Nome its first priority in Northwest Alaska.[19] As ever, Nomeites wished that their city were better connected to surrounding mining settlements, but by the early 1920s roads were better than they had been, and goods could be freighted over much of the Seward Peninsula.[20] As always, it was clear to Nomeites that the town needed a good road or train connection to interior Alaska—to Nenana, perhaps, and from there to Fairbanks, which by 1925 was called the Chicago of Alaska.[21]

Around this time, the government investigated the possibility of building a railroad line connecting Nome to Fairbanks or to Cook Inlet. But the distances involved and the demands of maintenance through mountains, valleys, and rivers and across unstable tundra made such schemes impractical.[22] At the end of the 1920s Nome's Chamber of Commerce endorsed the call of the International Highway Association, a Fairbanks group, for a road to that city from the contiguous states.[23] By this time, Nome enjoyed air service, so it had an economic interest in the prosperity of Fairbanks.

As was the case throughout the U.S. during the 1930s, public works put Nomeites to work. In 1936 alone nearly $111,000 was spent on Alaska Road Commission projects in the Seward Peninsula. Over $2,000 went to pay for streetlights in Nome and just over $800 for harbor lights. Work on a dock in Nome cost $3,000, improvements to the airfield at Nome $2,000. Almost $9,000 went toward improvements to the Nome–Council road, which up to that year had cost over $462,000 to build, improve, and maintain. To these were added projects on the Snake River, a wireless communications station, telephone lines, and a road to Teller. Given the material output of their region since 1899, Nomeites might have had reason to believe that they had not received their fair share of the some $16 million Congress had appropriated for public works in Alaska since 1905, along with Alaska's own contribution of $5 million. But Uncle Sam was hardly neglectful.[24]

In 1942, when the Soviet Union required American Lend–Lease material to fight the Germans, the federal government commissioned another study of potential railroad routes from Fairbanks to the Seward Peninsula. Then, too, the same old concerns, in addition to the length of time it would take to lay the tracks, along with the diminishing threat from German submarines to Soviet shipping, ended serious discussion of the program.[25] Fifteen years after the war Nomeites still hoped for—even expected—a Fairbanks road.[26] Some still did in the early twenty-first century.[27]

From the beginning, Nomeites had sought easier access to the interior and to other settlements on the Seward Peninsula. With equal consistency they had sought a harbor that would make Nome more accessible to sea traffic. Before and during the First World War their ardor for a harbor increased along with their hopes for prospective or growing industries—trade with Siberia, the production of reindeer meat, and fisheries, along with mining. Among the territorial legislature's first acts in 1913 was to ask the federal Congress to provide $25,000 for a survey to determine whether a harbor could be built at Nome. At the heart of this request was a belief, held by some Nomeites since 1900, that if a harbor were built, then businesses would come to the Seward Peninsula's metropolis. In 1913 the Alaska legislature emphasized the point by suggesting that business was being scared away from Nome by the costly wrecks of ships on its harborless coast. Even without a harbor, Nome had sent tens of millions of dollars in natural wealth to the Outside and over $10 million in goods had come into Nome. How much more, the legislature implied, would that trade increase if a harbor were built?[28] The response in Washington was disbelief in the practicality of the proposition.

The argument continued. In his 1916 campaign to be territorial delegate to the federal Congress, James Wickersham promised the Peninsula's voters that we would fight for a harbor, which, he said, Nomeites "ought to have."[29]

In the same year, a cumbersome headline on the front page of the recently renamed *Nome Tri-Weekly Nugget*—the slowing economy hurt this newspaper, too—expressed the city's ambition: "Banquet to Harbor Builders Discloses Deep Enthusiasm over Future Prospects of Seward Peninsula District." The eyebrow-raising fare—king salmon, steak, lamb chops, chicken, grapefruits, olives, potatoes, cheese, ice cream, cookies, and coffee—made for good feelings in keeping with high expectations.[30] The impressive menu also helped to make up for the negativity that had infused so much conversation about the harbor. In the opinion of Captain A. R. Ehrnbeck, Corps of Engineers, the natural conditions at Nome and the limited commerce there made a harbor unfeasible. A board of engineers concurred. Both were overruled by a superior who concluded that whatever boating traffic there was at Nome merited protection from the elements.[31]

Even as work on the harbor continued, officials in Washington, D.C., voiced skepticism. The cost of maintaining the harbor, about $25,000 a year, in addition to the costs of building it in the first place, was "out of all proportion to the benefits obtained,"[32] and even though the harbor that was built would be useful to Nome's fleet of small boats, it would never be suitable for large steamers.[33] The cost of shipping from Nome, moreover, was always prohibitive. From 1924 through 1935, each ton of goods shipped from Nome cost about $2.90. The cost of shipping the same tonnage in the state of Washington was about 10¢.

The city demonstrated its earnestness by offering to pay $2,500 annually for the harbor's upkeep; for several years the territorial government paid this in Nome's stead. Annual dredging was needed to keep the harbor open, adding to its costs.[34] As expected, damage from storms in 1936 and the mid-1940s made maintenance of the harbor all the more expensive.[35] From the time two jetties from the mouth of the Snake River that created a small harbor were completed through 1974, Nome paid had $127,000 for work on the harbor. In the same period, the federal government paid $4,552,000.

The harbor did make trade easier and safer. Already in the early fall of 1919 crews with Nome's "mosquito fleet"—traders in the Arctic and Siberia—took advantage of the Snake River Harbor.[36] But the first winter brought with it worries about the harbor's ability to withstand natural pressures. "Beautiful weather," Carl Lomen wrote in his diary in June of 1920. "Water commences running in Snake River. We are considering what effect the ice will have on the jetty."[37] Lomen, who was working to build a reindeer meat industry, had reason to be concerned: the harbor made exporting large shipments of reindeer meat—608 carcasses in September[38]—easier and less expensive, although never easy and cheap enough.[39]

HERDS

As the Russian Revolution and its aftermath were squelching the ambitions of Nome's traders, President Warren Harding visited Alaska. He was the first president to do so while in office and his death soon after the visit injected a sour note into commentary on it. Harding drove a golden spike into the ground at Nenana and thus symbolically completed the Alaska Railroad, but Nomeites were probably not surprised that his ensuing speech about Alaska was given in Seattle. Nor was it remarkable that Harding paid tribute to Alaska's railroad workers. Nomeites, of all Alaskans, knew what dreams workable railroads could fulfill. In his speech the President had also said he was stunned, as every feeling person must be, at Alaska's natural beauty. Each turn seemed to bring with it a view more spectacular than the last, he said. And, as always, Alaska evoked imperial musings: Alaska was an "enchanting empire," a "great Northwestern Empire," an "empire of scenic wonders."

But Harding never came within five hundred miles of Nome. Save for the negative example of the bad old days when wild miners ruled the land, Nome figured in his speech not at all. Aside from mining, the industries the president promoted—pulp manufacture, salmon, and oil—were far removed from Nome's concerns.[40] Pulp demanded trees—a nonstarter for Nomeites—and no oil discoveries had been made in the region. And while fishing was good for local sport and consumption,[41] the challenge of getting fish to market in the lower states was too great. Talk about making Nome a center for Alaska fisheries never moved beyond hype and theory.[42]

Aside from gold mining, the one industry that mattered, in the sense that it could keep Nome in America's mind, involved reindeer. As Judge Lomen said (with his customary hyperbole) in the unpublished book *In Reindeer Realms*, the Seward Peninsula's managed herds would "reclaim barren wastes and frozen tundras surpassing in extent the empires founded by Alexander the Great and Genghis Khan."[43] In another, more grounded speech Lomen said that the reindeer herds would make possible a permanent population over wide areas of the far north that otherwise would remain all but uninhabited.[44] Vilhjalmur Stefansson, a popular writer and friend of the Lomen family, wrote in 1924 that the far north was on the point of becoming the largest meat-producing area on the globe "and eventually the only area where meat is produced on a large scale."[45] Once again, Nome seemed poised to have global influence.

Certainly, the reindeer trade contributed to the Seward Peninsula's internationalism. In the early 1920s Carl Lomen inquired into the possibility of raising reindeer on Wrangel Island, which was occupied by Canadians and, later, by the Soviets.[46] Herds on the Seward Peninsula were driven by Lapps, Natives, and, in time, undifferentiated "whites" under the direction of the Lomens. The reindeer had first been brought to Alaska in the late nineteenth century from Siberia to provide food and employment to Natives.[47] According to a report from the Alaskan Education Bureau, the introduction of reindeer into Alaska provided Natives with a practical industry that trained members of "a primitive race into independence and responsible citizenship."[48] Carl Lomen sought to make the reindeer trade a rationalized, organized, and cost-effective industry. In 1927 the Lomen Reindeer Corporation was established under the laws of Delaware,[49] and it had distributors in Seattle, Portland, Minneapolis and St. Paul, Oklahoma City, Chicago, New York, and Boston. The daunting task was getting the meat to them—not an easy thing when it needed to be shipped three thousand miles on refrigerated ships.[50] Of course, the costs involved in getting the meat to markets in the Outside was passed on to consumers. In 1921, beef in New York sold wholesale for about 21 cents per pound, while a pound of reindeer cost between 35 and 40 cents.[51]

Marketing the product was easier than shipping and selling it. Following the revelations of Upton Sinclair's *The Jungle* (1905) and other works shedding light on the filthy conditions of the urban meat industry, reindeer meat was attractive to consumers who could afford it. Reindeer could, perhaps, be for them what "free-range" meat was to health-conscious diners ninety years later. Elegant mammals running free on the tundra evoked feelings of exotic cleanliness,[52] and Lomen sought to capitalize on the romance of arctic victuals by supplying large department stores in the U.S. with live reindeer to accompany neighborhood

Santa Clauses.[53] Friendly writers penned articles on Alaska's reindeer,[54] although, unfortunately for the Lomens, the children's books *Smoozie: The Story of an Alaskan Reindeer Fawn* (1941), *Littlest Reindeer* (1946), and *Reindeer Trail* (1959) were too late to be of help.

The reindeer industry was important to the Seward Peninsula's non-Natives conceptually and potentially; it was cited several times as a justification for the costs of further work on Nome's harbor,[55] and it provided a staple of Nomeites' diet, making the consumption of beef in the city by 1924 negligible.[56] But the reindeer business had little economic impact on Nome. Carl Lomen's memoir, *Fifty Years in Alaska*, tells us some things about Nome but there are no indications that the reindeer industry had an effect on the city's day-to-day experience. Government reports on the reindeer herds provide little useful information about the city.[57]

In a very minor way, this dearth of influence reflects racial views. Through the first few decades of the twentieth century some Nomeites had sought to minimize or control the presence of Natives. Of the hundreds of photographs of Natives from the Nome region, very few show Natives within the city's limits, and in the late summer of 1903 the *Nome Nugget* complained about Natives "hanging about the stores and saloons, learning plenty of vice and little good." It was not long before a twenty-acre voluntary reservation of sorts was established at the mouth of Quartz Creek, twenty miles west of Nome, partly to prevent Natives from being debauched by Nome's majority population, and partly—and simply—to get the Natives out of town. In 1906 a similar operation was initiated seven miles further west.[58] Many of the Natives who still came into town did so only in the summer months, to fish and to sell handicrafts, although a few sold crab there in the winter.[59] Thus, the fact that the Lomens' operation overwhelmingly employed Natives—nearly six hundred in 1929 as opposed to seventy non-Natives—meant that the business's effect on its employees would not have much of a direct effect on Nome.[60] The reindeer meat eaten in Nome, moreover, was herded by Natives, not by the Lomens.[61] Thus, for some Nomeites the reindeer industry was a Native entity and that placed a psychological barrier between it and them. The reindeer trade shaped how they viewed their Alaskan world and they benefited from it nutritionally. But they also seemed to hold the reindeer trade at a mental distance, save for the few, such as Carl Lomen, who had a vested interest in it.[62]

Much more important in explaining the industry's slim effect on Nome were practical concerns. The Lomens never found a way to make shipments of reindeer to the U.S. market cost-effective. When the Depression struck in 1929 and fewer customers were willing to pay higher prices for reindeer than for other meats, this challenge became more daunting. Add to this the efforts of Outside meat producers who launched an expensive newspaper campaign against the Lomen business, and allegations by government officials that the so-called Nome reindeer herd was "demoralized" because its careless tenders "wanted to spend their time in the poolrooms of the town," and the wonder is that the Lomens stuck with the business through most of the 1930s.[63]

To suggest that the reindeer business had little effect on Nome's economy is not to say that the reindeer trade was insubstantial. On September 28, 1920, almost two hundred deer were shipped from Nome on the S.S. *Ketchikan;* twenty days later one thousand additional deer were shipped from the city.[64] In 1927 the Lomens sent 277 tons of reindeer meat to the U.S. The next year the figure leaped to 832 tons.[65] But the labor needed to get this done was accomplished by a small number of workers, some of whom did not live in Nome for long periods. The Lomens' facilities in Nome were built by laborers from the Outside and their company lightered its own goods.[66] And, anyway, not many Nomeites were needed to get reindeer carcasses onto ships.

So the end of the Lomens' reindeer industry came as a blow to Nome, but the blow was more psychological than economic. The end came in September of 1937 when President Roosevelt signed a bill passed by both houses of Congress, and the Lomens (with all non-Natives) were banned from reindeer herding. "The reindeer industry was now to become purely an Eskimo business, with whites, Lapps, and others forever barred."[67] The government's position—helped along by anti-reindeer (i.e., pro-cattle) lobbyists and paternalistic government agents—was that the reindeer herds should be reserved for Native consumption and economic betterment. (The Canadian government, which acquired nearly twenty-four hundred reindeer from the Lomens in 1935, did not have similar qualms, perhaps because Canadian cattle and sheep herders did not protest.)[68]

PRELUDE TO ASHES

Storms punctuated life in Nome from the start, and a few of them were devastating. The fire of mid-September 1905 annihilated two city blocks—about fifty businesses and twenty cabins.[69] The storm and flood of 1913, captured in at least two hundred photographs, ripped ocean vessels from their moorings and cast the *Sawtooth of Nome* high on the shore. This storm inundated some homes completely, splintered others, and decimated a large portion of Front Street. The body language of cleanup crews beholding the scene seemed to ask, where to begin?[70] But Nome was rebuilt, and more storms came.

Fire, too, wreaked ruin, first in 1901 and again in 1905. The greatest of all Nome's fires struck on September 17, 1934. For Nomeites thereafter, this was *the* fire. Four years after it, the editor of a collection of Nome writing divided B.F. texts from A.F. texts—articles written before and after the fire.[71]

The flames of 1934 devastated an ordinary, frumpy place. By the Northwestern Alaska Chamber of Commerce's own admission, a number of buildings in Nome had been abandoned, and "in many ways the town has the outward appearance of a 'has been.'"[72] Such honesty placed where less truthful marketing might have been is impressive in its own way. It suggests that Nome's residents were comfortable with what their city had become. If outsiders did not like the town the way it was, no one was begging them to visit. And, anyway, there was still much in Nome to appreciate. As we have seen, air travel was available there year-round. Roust Airways, with bases at Nome and Candle, invited patrons to fly in its comfortably heated cabins. Its competitors, Pacific Alaska Airways and the Mirow Air Service, also had bases there. The city had boasted a well-equipped hospital and three churches. The Pioneers of Alaska and Arctic Brotherhood sponsored libraries. Local chickens provided fresh eggs, and youngsters "thrived" on canned food and milk. A higher percentage of children attended public schools in Nome than in the States. Nomeites enjoyed skating, skiing, parties, dances, and amateur theatricals. "Surf bathing may sound unreasonable but is not uncommon."[73]

The last issue of the *Nugget* to appear before its office was destroyed was published on Saturday, September 15. It revealed a city immersed in American ordinariness.[74] The front page announced a textile strike in the Outside and informed readers that U.S. Revenue Department cutters were searching for a Japanese fishing boat whose crew had attacked three Filipino police officers. Meanwhile, a Chinese delegate to the League of Nations had warned that there was "abundant evidence of danger of a war in the far east which would be closely and inseparably linked with the peace prospects of Europe." This was hardly prescient; Japan and China were already at war and Japan presented a threat to American, British, Dutch, French, and Russian holdings in Asia.

But the delegate's claim went against the grain of European leaders for whom "appeasement" was still an unloaded word. Nomeites had been warning of war in Asia for over thirty years. Americans generally, on the other hand, were almost completely uninterested in foreign affairs—understandably, perhaps, given the country's immersion in an economic depression that would endure into 1940. When war finally came to America and, with the attack on Dutch Harbor and the far western Aleutians, to Alaska, there was the hope that the economic assistance Fort Davis had brought to Nome in earlier decades would be experienced anew. ("History shows that permanent development follows the United States Army wherever it goes," the *Nugget* reported after the Japanese attack on Pearl Harbor. "History is at present repeating itself—this time in Alaska.")[75]

On September 15, 1934, the *Nugget's* second page said that the S.S. *Victoria* had left Seattle on September 13 and was due to arrive soon. Most in Nome knew and some remembered from personal experience that in 1918 the *"Vic"* had brought devastating flu to Nome. Carl Lomen's diary provides a rudimentary chronicle. October 19: "Many under some sort of spell"; October 20: "The army post in quarantine. Schools closed, movies, Churches, etc."; October 28: "We fear the influenza, now raging through the States"; November 6, while aboard the *Victoria* en route to Seattle: "Many of the *Vic* passengers seriously ill." By November 15, 23 passengers aboard the *Victoria* had died as had some 165 in Nome. Within a week, 35 on the ship were gone, and the toll in Nome had risen to over 200. Memories of these figures might have helped Nomeites in the fall of 1934 to place events in some perspective. According to the first reports, just two were killed by the fire.[76] Later accounts reported none were killed or injured.

In other news, *Platinum Blonde*, starring Jean Harlow, Robert Williams, and Loretta Young, was playing at Nome's Dream Theatre; a lieutenant with the U.S. Signal Corps was making inspections at Nome's signal station; and the *Nugget's* comics page featured strips of "The Featherheads," "Finney of the Force," "S'matter Pop," and "Keeping Up with the Joneses." As if to celebrate the national demise of prohibition the previous year, the Bon Marché store's grocery department offered great reductions in liquor prices. Beer cost 15 cents a pint.

On September 15, 1934, Nome's mothers learned about a new study suggesting that infants raised in private homes were afraid of snakes while those raised in hospitals were not. Jean Newton, the child-raising expert—a member of the relatively new class of person on the American scene, courtesy of the young disciplines of psychology and sociology—admonished readers to stop inculcating irrational fears, such as of snakes, into their children. Perhaps this struck Nome's readers as comical. The list of things to fear in Nome—uncontrolled fires, for instance, and frostbite—had been written at the behest of experience. Snakes had never been a problem.

For some, particularly those opposed to the growing economic activism of the Roosevelt administration, taxes *were* a problem. The day's political cartoon showed an elderly man drowning, up to his neck in taxes. In a few days, when the wheels of federal relief began to turn for the benefit of Nome, the cartoon's message might have seemed inapt. This was Saturday.

On Sunday, as on every Sabbath, the town was quieter. Few worked; the presses at the newspaper were silent. Nome's Catholics and Protestants went to their respective churches at peace with one another, partly because of the general easygoingness of the town's subculture, and partly because theological differences had never mattered very much in Nome, at least not in public.

FLAMES

The fire began at about 10:30 Monday morning.[77] As with the fire of 1901, this one started in the Golden Gate Hotel. The flames were helped along by strong winds that, according to various accounts, blew at between twenty-five and forty miles per hour.[78] With buildings so close together, the fire department could do nothing substantial. Before long, its own facilities and equipment were destroyed.

At the outset, people gathered on both sides of the hotel to see what they could do. Some put up a ladder to help a few of the guests escape from a burning building. Others tried to get food out of the grocery stores and medicinal goods out of pharmacies before they burned. As the situation became hopeless, many just watched.[79] Early reports said the population was in danger of starvation, but although much was lost, most of what Nomeites had already set aside in preparation for winter was saved, as was a six-hundred-ton shipment of goods that had been brought to Nome by the *Victoria* in late August.[80]

The federal courthouse and jail burned. The offices of the Alaska Road Commission, the government reindeer service, and the Bureau of Indian Affairs burned. Nome's customs house, the post office, and Coast Guard boathouse burned.[81] Countless records of historical interest—trial papers, business documents, memoranda, and photograph collections—burned.[82] The Miners and Merchants Bank and the Weather Bureau burned. The Lincoln Hotel, garages, pool rooms, and saloons burned. Residences on Front Street and adjacent lanes burned. "The flames swept a path ten blocks long and three blocks wide through the heart of town, virtually wiping it out."[83] In all, sixty-five businesses and ninety homes were destroyed.[84] Of Nome's 1,200 to 1,500 residents, 400 were left homeless. Early accounts in the *New York Times* and elsewhere first reported that all Nomeites were without homes.[85] The fire had done most of its damage by early afternoon, although it smoldered through the night. Ralph Lomen sent a telegram to his brother Carl, then in New York, estimating losses at between two and three million dollars.[86]

The next day the Coast Guard cutter *Chelan* began making its way from Dutch Harbor to Nome, where it would meet the *Northland*, which was based at the city. Other cutters along the U.S. West Coast were alerted that they also might need to steam north. The territorial government put out a call for federal assistance. Within two days, radio technicians and representatives from the Bureau of Commerce and Alaska Road Commission flew to the city. In Anchorage, food and medical supplies were readied for shipment; in Seattle, the Alaska Steamship Company reduced its freight rates to Nome by half;[87] in Pittsburgh, Eleanor Roosevelt expressed sympathy; in Washington, D.C., the Federal Emergency Relief Administration made $50,000 available; and in Nome, it rained.[88]

This was not the time for clichés, but they seemed unavoidable and, to the extent they were noticed, they were probably comforting. "Fires may be quenched," the *Seward Gateway* noted, "but not the unconquerable spirit of the pioneers who built Nome and pushed back the lonely Alaska wilderness."[89] Inevitably, Nome was likened to the archetypal phoenix springing from a sea of flames.[90]

For the only time in Nome since the beginning of the gold rush, the town had no formal newspaper. In its place came a Federal Emergency Relief Administration Bulletin. It focused on rebuilding efforts and added some daily news under the heading of the *Nugget*. The work of the federal government was organized under the roof of the old Pioneer Mining Company building.

The old saying is that people should be careful about what they ask for since they might get it. For decades Nomeites had cried for more government attention. Now they had it; the rebuilding of Nome was mostly financed by the Federal Emergency Relief Administration, an early New Deal program that would soon be folded into the Public Works Administration.[91] The $50,000 FERA gave to Nome was the sum Governor John Troy proposed to Harold Ickes of the Department of the Interior.[92] The funds put Nomeites to work clearing debris and rebuilding. By the end of September, Troy had orchestrated a telegram-sending campaign asking for an additional $250,000 from the PWA. The future Alaska governor and U.S. Senator, Ernest Gruening, was now director of the Territories and Island Possessions division of the Interior Department, and he received notes from chambers of commerce in Los Angeles, San Francisco, and Portland, as well as from various Alaska pioneer clubs, urging the government to release PWA monies.[93]

Receiving relief from government bureaucracies and their agents was one thing. For most in Nome, it was more difficult to accept help from the Red Cross, which expended $23,000 in Nome building thirteen homes and providing residents with food, clothing, and replacements for lost equipment. Nome's population, the Red Cross's official summary noted, was "instinctively reluctant to accept outside help."[94] A week after the fire, the Red Cross's man on the spot, Bowen McCoy, reported that Nomeites who needed help avoided him. He was able to discover what the Red Cross could do there only after intensive effort.[95] By all accounts, Nome's population was brave, stoic, and cool. Residents whose homes had not burned opened them to those who had. There is no evidence that the consequent shrinkage of personal space led to frayed nerves. Outsiders wondered at how, after the city collapsed, its residents simply determined that they would start over.[96]

The Lomens' lighterage facilities and warehouses, along with the Pioneer Mining Company, were among the few businesses still standing. The Lomen family made these available to the government.[97] Perhaps they hoped this gesture would influence the government to favor reindeer herds owned by non-Natives. The Lomens also owned a reindeer herd near Nome, which could be used for food if needed. But more than by enlightened self-interest, the Lomens were motivated by a desire to lend a hand to a town their family had done so much to build up. Along with other businessmen, state officials, and Nome's mayor, Alfred Lomen served on the rebuilding committee that was organized immediately after the fire.[98] Once again, the Lomens proved themselves an unusually public-minded family.

Coming as it did in the depths of the Great Depression, some understandably saw the devastation of Nome as an opportunity. Two weeks after the fire, Paul Ziedler of Mount Vernon, New York, wrote to the Interior Department "desirous of ascertaining the possibility of employment in the rebuilding of Nome." The following spring the Colorado State Emergency Relief Administration inquired whether residents of that state might find employment in Nome.[99] Ernest Harrison of Joliet, Illinois, a veteran and father of four who had been out of work since 1931, also hoped to land a job in Nome. He sent three separate letters of inquiry.[100] Henry Ziehl of Baltimore, too, wanted to go to Nome.[101] And B. M. Schorn of Minneapolis had heard a rumor that the government intended to repopulate Nome. If so, he was interested in getting work there.[102] Bureaucrats at the Interior Department advised all of these not to go to the Seward Peninsula. No more workers were needed in Nome and, in any case, Alaskans would be favored for employment over outsiders.

For a brief time, in some quarters, there was informal talk in the Public Works Administration about relocating Nome's population to Teller, the site of the Seward Peninsula's only natural harbor. Meanwhile, the Interior Department's R. A. Kleindienst advised against rebuilding Nome with permanent homes. He expected the town to die within a few years.[103] Against both plans stood Nome's infrastructure, actual and anticipated, and the will of its inhabitants. The *Nugget* drove this point home. When it began publishing again

FIGURE 15. *"Storm 1934," Lomen Family Collection, no number, Archives, Alaska and Polar Regions Department, University of Alaska Fairbanks.*

in November it announced atop its front page: "Nome is the Strategic World Flight Air Base."

As winter descended, the *Nugget*'s editor, former mayor George Maynard, reminded Nomeites what they had to be thankful for. The "razing of old, time-worn, eye-sores, and the burning down of potential fire-traps, may be a God-send to this city."[104] The paper acknowledged that among the fire's collateral casualties were the Arctic Brotherhood (disbanded) and the Lomen Brothers' pharmacy (not to be rebuilt). But even this latter news contained a golden message for the Nome Drug Store, which would not close. The drugstore joined the Nome Machine Shop, Nome Laundry, Nome Motor Company, and Nome Harbor and Lighterage Company in resurrecting the town.

And if a newspaperman's musings can be taken as representative, the fire seems to have spurred religious revival. For the first time since the town's

FIGURE 16. *"Nome aerial," Lomen Family Collection, acc. no. 72-71-1594, Archives, Alaska and Polar Regions Department, University of Alaska Fairbanks.*

beginning, vaporous Christmastide musings were abandoned for the sake of something approaching genuine reflection. "[R]egardless of the rest of the world at this particular moment, Nome has a heart full of joyousness and thankfulness for the Blessings which [God] has bestowed upon us during the past year, in the name of Jesus Christ."[105] The article included a rendition of the Lord's Prayer.

After rebuilding, the most obvious change was the town's new look. Multistory buildings were no longer built close together on narrow lanes. Front Street was broadened and spaces were placed between buildings. The town looked fundamentally different. The resurrected Front Street, unlike earlier reconstructions following fires or storms, had lost its partly Edwardian, partly western look. In this new Nome, there were no buildings to rival the Golden Gate Hotel. The post office and bank appeared merely functional. There was nothing about them to make contemporary photographers pay attention.[106]

CONCLUSION

I would like to say I'm proud of the pioneer people of Nome and what they accomplished. Coming into an environment more alien to the very great majority than the moon is to us today, they set up their government and an American civilization in that environment and tried to give their children the same education and advantages they would have received "Outside."

—Irving Reed, 1969

In the years after the fire of 1934, Nome experienced more disasters, which, although less catastrophic, led to more federal assistance. A breakwater, designed to keep storm waves from Front Street, was funded by the government and completed in 1950; the territorial legislature had first asked for one in 1917.[1] Seventy years after the fire, no devastation remotely comparable had struck the city. Safety measures worked.

After rebuilding, life in Nome carried on as it had before. In the 1950s, the Grant Creek Mining Company and the Kotzebue Gold Dust Mining Company plowed the tundra. The Lomen Commercial Company remained in Nome, although its operations had expanded to Juneau, Fairbanks, and Anchorage.[2] The Northern Commercial Company, which had returned to Nome in 1939 after thirty-six years away, owned two of Nome's forty stores, employed twenty of its eighteen hundred citizens, and was the Seward Peninsula's Ford automobile dealer. The Company conducted $600,000 of business in 1939, and, we are told, its Nome manager arrived there at the height of his merchandizing career and was enjoying a pleasant life.[3] Before long, the city looked to tourism for income.[4]

By the early 1940s Pan American Airlines flew a Fairbanks–Nome route three times weekly and telegrams from Nome to the Outside cost $2, the same as from Anchorage, Fairbanks, and Kodiak. The basic economic goods Nome's Americans expected in the early 1940s cost about $3,123 annually, slightly less than the cost of living in Fairbanks ($3,223) and not much more than that of Anchorage ($2,816). The cost of building a home in Nome was no more expensive than in Fairbanks, and minimum monthly house rentals were cheaper in Nome than in Fairbanks, Sitka, and Seward.[5] And, although as of 1951 Nome's

Pioneers of Alaska were far outnumbered by the club at Fairbanks (200 to 640), the Nome club was much larger than the organizations in Anchorage (79) and Nenana (21). The club's territory-wide presidency was held by Nomeites in 1933 (Alfred Lomen) and 1947 (Antonio Polet).[6]

In the years following the fire, themes like some of those that had appeared in Nome's early newspaper commentary showed up elsewhere in Alaska. One of these was that colonizers by the hundreds of thousands—even millions—were on the way to Alaska. The same day it reported fire in Nome, the *Anchorage Daily News* announced a scheme to resettle a million black Americans in the territory. In addition to liberating the colonizers from discrimination in the States, the plan's promoter claimed, such a settlement would prevent a Japanese invasion of America.[7] As Nome's promoters had observed years before, a settled Alaska would be a less inviting target to Asian aggressors. This was the latest contribution to thought about black resettlement, musings on which went back to the eighteenth century with advocates as different as James Madison, John Marshall, James Monroe, Abraham Lincoln, and Marcus Garvey. A few years later rumors circulated that a large number of Mormons were planning to settle in the Matanuska Valley. Yet another proposal, entertained by the secretary of state in Washington, D.C., among others, was that Jews suffering persecution in Nazi Germany could be settled in Alaska. Alaskans agreed that the territory needed more inhabitants, and the Mormons had proved themselves in Utah, in San Bernardino, California, and elsewhere. But the prospective Jewish newcomers were, they thought, of the wrong kind.

Resistance to Jewish settlement had partly to do with an underlying, if not always malicious, anti-Semitism that was the norm in the Western world before the Second World War. The memoirs of Nome's famous dog musher, A. A. "Scotty" Allan, include a reference to "Oofty . . . a queer-looking little Jew."[8] Allan meant no harm, but his fixation on Jews—he commented on several Alaskans' Jewishness—and the belittling language he used when writing about them, were, at the time, ubiquitous traits in the U.S. and Canada, in western Europe, and, much more viciously, in central and eastern Europe. Grimmer are the memories of Julia Scully, a New York editor, who lived in Nome during the Second World War. Late in life she remembered students in Nome denouncing "dirty Kikes" as well as an upper-class woman going to extremes not to let her Jewish housekeeper leave through the front door.[9] In the main, though, Alaskans opposed to the resettlement scheme thought that Germany's Jews were the wrong sort to succeed in Alaska. As Nome's writers had said before, so other Alaskans said now: genteel urbanites with soft hands were not the kind to make an empire of Alaska. Moreover, Germany's "Jewish problem" was not Alaska's to solve, the *Fairbanks Daily News-Miner* noted in late 1938, unaware of how ghoulish the observation would sound in a few years. What Alaska needed were "people schooled in American traditions and such as she can assimilate and with whom she can build from the ground up with security and solidarity."[10]

More dramatic was the fulfillment in the mid-twentieth century of early Nomeite prophesies. The Second World War brought home the point that Nome's residents had been making for decades, namely, that Alaska was strategically significant and required a military infrastructure. During the war, an airbase built at Nome was used by Soviet pilots carrying Lend–Lease goods to Russia.[11] In 1942 the long-feared invasion from Japan came, albeit on the very distant Aleutian Islands of Attu and Kiska. Three years before there had been 500 American sailors and soldiers in Alaska; by 1943 there were 152,000.[12] As Nome's first editorialists had said repeatedly, Alaska was essential to the projection of American power into the Pacific. They would have approved of the claim, made in 1943 by a leading journalist, Joseph Driscoll, that in some sense Alaska *is* America.[13]

By the fall of 1934 it was clear that Nome's day as Alaska's leading city had passed. In an undated speech given to the Seaview Women's Club of West Seattle, Ralph Lomen called Fairbanks Alaska's "golden heart" but, curiously, never mentioned Nome.[14] By the mid-1930s, this kind of benign inattention was common. In many books on Alaska—*The Gold Fever* (1923), *Chechahco and Sourdough* (1926), *Grit, Grief and Gold* (1933), *Alaska Holiday* (1940), *Alaska Beckons* (1947), *Alaska: Land of Tomorrow* (1947), *Rugged Years on the Alaska Frontier* (1949), and *Arctic Mood* (1949)—Nome is only briefly alluded to or, more commonly, passed over altogether. One memoirist, writing forty years after the fact, recalled his days in Nome as the best of his life, yet he admitted never to have visited the city after leaving it.[15]

As always, Nome the symbol vied for attention with Nome the real American settlement. A late-twentieth-century historian focused on the city mainly to praise its inhabitants' sheer endurance: Nomeites' perseverance through storm, fire, and arctic hardship made Nome a "quintessential Alaskan" town.[16] But, fourteen years later, the same author would hardly notice Nome in an overview of Alaska history; references to the city were restricted to the gold rush era; the *Nome Nugget*, Alaska's most enduring newspaper, does not find a place in the author's bibliography among the *Fairbanks Daily News-Miner*, the *Anchorage Times*, and the *Ketchikan Chronicle*.[17]

Indeed, by the 1950s, there was a widespread, if implicit, agreement that Nome's significance lay in the first few years of its life. A widely used text, published for the second time in 1987, notes that the coming of airplanes to Nome mitigated its isolation and that Nomeites felt they had been allotted too few state troopers after Alaska became a state in 1959; otherwise, the book's comments on Nome are restricted to the gold boom.[18] A more recent history of Alaska had additional things to say of post–gold rush Nome—it mentions airplanes, the serum run of 1925, and fears that Nome might be attacked during the Second World War—but the emphasis remained on the gold rush, and the language of the book is replete with the kind of inflated *behold-the-Alaskans'-derring-do* rhetoric that has dominated writing about Alaska since the late nineteenth century.[19]

Nomeites were themselves complicit in promoting this limited vision. Already by the mid-1940s the city was being advertised, rather incredibly, as a place that had hardly changed since gold-rush days.[20] City letterhead used fifty years later announced that the city was "celebrating 100 years of Gold Rush History," and informational signs posted near Nome for the sake of tourists focused almost entirely on the gold-rush era. To the person interested in more than Nome's first few years, the city might have appeared to be little more than a sometime boomtown that lingered just because people happened to live there.[21]

As for the quality of life in the city, visitors and memoirists did not agree. One enthusiastic traveler described Nome as a "gallant city," full of busy elderly people, with homes that enjoyed rudimentary but functional plumbing, hand lotion, ink, and Kleenex. At the same time, we read, mail-order goods were difficult to get in a timely way, the cost of living was high, and chances for year-round employment were low. Older Natives found it difficult to adapt to city life, although Native teenagers were doing well in school. Meantime, over fifty gold operations shipped their goods from Nome, a bleak, muddy place where, nevertheless, companionship bound "arctic-dwellers" together.[22] This mixed but generally positive account was offset by the observations of another writer who noted that parts of Nome struck him as more abject than anything he had seen in Africa, Latin America, India, and other places in the Third World.[23] Yet another described the city as a "warm and friendly" place where an "almost tropical lassitude" prevailed, where dogs and children ran free in the streets, where the formerly gold-soaked beaches were now littered with cans and bottles.[24]

Julia Scully is more pointed, recalling the Nome of her childhood as "a few rows of shacks," a "bleak and comfortless place," a gathering place for drunks and indifferent teachers. Nome, Scully recalls, was a "hellhole," the "end of the earth," "nowheresville." In the 1940s, Scully says, Nome's white high school students did not even consider the possibility of learning about Eskimo culture, less from a sense of contempt for Natives than from a desire to distance themselves from their identity as Nomeites and to fashion themselves after what they saw in glossy magazines.[25]

It was true that Nome's Dream Theatre was segregated—in practice, not legally—through the 1940s.[26] But segregation soon broke down. As always, children played together without regard to complexion,[27] and Natives needed merchants just as merchants needed customers. In a place so challenging and precarious, so buffeted by the elements and at the mercy of outsiders, internal strife did not make sense. The region's Natives and non-Natives had had a mutual influence upon one another since the beginning of continual contact.[28] Thus, as years passed, a quiet alteration took place without violence and with little rancor. By mid-century over one-quarter of Nome's residents were Natives, and William E. Beltz was elected from among them to the territorial legislature in 1948, and then to its senate two years later.[29]

FIGURE 17. *The road from Council to Nome, 2003. Photo by author.*

This book's final words are left to a local, the owner of a café on Front Street I spoke with in Nome in the summer of 2004. As she talked about her hometown, I heard echoes of things that had been written a hundred years before. I took notes. "We need roads," she said. "Harbor needs to be expanded." "Population fluctuates—a lot of transience—new faces come and go." "Maybe need a railroad to Fairbanks." "Maybe gold industry will come back." "Takes a certain type of person to live here." "Tough."

NOTES

PREFACE

1.   Alfred J. Lomen, "Reflections," *Aurora* (Nome, Alaska: Nome High School, 1915), 20.

INTRODUCTION

1   In addition to the secondary sources I cite in chapter 1, see, for example, William R. Hunt, *North of 53: The Wild Days of the Alaska–Yukon Mining Frontier* (New York: Macmillan, 1974), 95–135; and David B. Wharton, *The Alaska Gold Rush* (Bloomington: Indiana Univ. Press, 1972), 178–210.

2   For demographic information about the first Nomeites see James H. Ducker, "Gold-Rushers to the North: The People of Nome in 1900," unpublished paper, 1977, 4.

3   A. A. "Scotty" Allan, *Gold, Men and Dogs* (New York: G. P. Putnam's Sons, 1931), 5.

4   George Edward Adams, "Cape Nome's Wonderful Placer Mines," *Harper's Weekly*, June 9, 1900, 529.

5   In a different article, George Edward Adams maintained that "Cape Nome certainly presented many novel features entirely new to the mind." See his "Cape Nome Beach and Tundra Placer Mines," *Harper's Weekly*, August 4, 1900, 724.

6   Many of the Lomens' pictures survive in museum and archive collections throughout Alaska and at the Glenbow Museum in Calgary.

7   Vilhjalmur Stefansson, *The Adventure of Wrangel Island* (New York: Macmillan, 1924), xvi, 133, 138.

8   Vilhjalmur Stefansson, *Northwest to Fortune: The Search of Western Man for a Commercially Practical Route to the Far East* (New York: Duell, Sloan and Pearce, 1958), 321.

9   Vilhjalmur Stefansson, *Discovery: The Autobiography of Vilhjalmur Stefansson* (New York: McGraw-Hill, 1964), 267, 309, 353–54.

10   Carl J. Lomen, *Fifty Years in Alaska* (New York: David McKay, 1954), 67.

11   Adams, "Cape Nome's Wonderful Placer Mines," 530.

12   *Aurora*, 1914, 54. By 1920 47 percent of college students were women. See Christopher J. Lucas, *American Higher Education: A History* (New York: St. Martin's Griffin, 1994), 206.

13   This section of the introduction draws heavily from Preston Jones, "Yankees in Parkas: Native Influence at Nome, 1900–1920," *Alaska History* 20, no. 2 (Fall 2005): 43–58.

14   George Edward Adams wrote that the settlers at Nome were "thoroughly imbued with Yankee ingenuity and push." See his "Cape Nome Beach and Tundra Placer Mines," 724. On condescending language, see Marius Hansome, "The Eskimo and the Fourth 'R'," *Current History* 16, April 22, 1922, 103, 107.

15   *Nome Nugget* quoted in Donald Craig Mitchell, *Sold American: The Story of Alaska Natives and Their Land, 1867–1959* (Hanover, NH: Univ. Press of New England, 1997), 144.

16   Helen Kreps, "The Eskimo of Alaska" *Aurora*, 1915, 6.

17   Psychologist Spencer Rathus defines projection as "a defense mechanism in which unacceptable ideas and impulses are cast out or attributed to others." See his *Psychology in the New Millennium*, 7th edition (Fort Worth: Harcourt Brace, 1999), G20.

18   Mitchell, *Sold American*, 143–48. However, Mitchell relies too heavily on the *Nugget* (1903–1905) to make general claims.

19   *Nome Nugget*, April 7, 1917.

20   Kreps, "Eskimo of Alaska."

21   *Daily Nome Industrial Worker*, April 5, 1917.

22   Stefansson, *Adventure of Wrangel Island*, 112.

23   Jennifer Niven, *Ada Blackjack: A True Story of Survival in the Arctic* (New York: Hyperion, 2003), 8, 365, and 368.

24   Mitchell, *Sold American*, 143–48.

25   T. A. Rickard, *Through the Yukon and Alaska* (San Francisco: Mining and Scientific Press, 1909), 318; and Irving McKenny Reed, *Boyhood in the Nome Gold Camp* (College, AK: Mineral Industry Research Laboratory, 1969), 24.

26   *Nome Daily Gold Digger*, October 31, 1906: "[T]he reservation idea does not appeal very strongly to us, [but] it would seem that none better offers itself at this time."

27   Charles Madsen, *Arctic Trader* (New York: Dodd, Mead, 1957), 3; Lomen, *Fifty Years in Alaska*, 61, 64, 66; *Nome Industrial Worker*, April 11, 1917; and John W. Krug and Caryl Sale Krug, *One Dog Short: The Odyssey and Collection of a Family in Alaska during the Gold Rush* (Juneau: Alaska Department of Education, 1998), 139.

28   Rickard, *Through the Yukon and Alaska*, 314.

29   *Nome Industrial Worker*, April 11, 1917.

30   See the photographs in Krug and Krug, *One Dog Short*, 78–79, 141; Reed, *Boyhood in the Nome Gold Camp*, 25; and Frank G. Carpenter, *Alaska, Our Northern Wonderland* (New York: Doubleday, Page, 1925), 189.

31   See, for another example, the photograph on the inside cover of the 1915 edition of Nome High School's *Aurora*.

32   Lomen, *Fifty Years in Alaska*, 36.

33   See the inside cover of Mary Lee Davis, *Uncle Sam's Attic: The Intimate Story of Alaska* (Boston: Wilde, 1930).

34   See the photographs of the drivers in Nome Kennel Club, "All Alaska Sweepstakes, 1910"; the photograph in Louise Anita Martin, *North to Nome* (Chicago: Albert Whitman, 1939), 287; and Rickard, *Through the Yukon and Alaska*, 319.

35   E. S. Harrison, "Alaska Basketball Team Touring the United States," n.p., n.d., 7.

36   Evangeline Atwood, *Frontier Politics: Alaska's James Wickersham* (Portland, OR: Binford and Mort, 1979), 94.

37   See the photograph in the Lomen Family Photograph Collection, Box 8, folder 119.

38   See *Nome Gold Digger*, February 7, 1900; February 28, 1900.

39   Madsen, *Arctic Trader*, 10–11.

40   *Nome Gold Digger*, February 14, 1900.

41   *Nome Daily Gold Digger*, October 31, 1906.

42   Kreps, "Eskimo of Alaska," 5.

43   Rickard, *Through the Yukon and Alaska*, 319–20.

44   For an overview, see "The Age of Gold," in Paula Mitchell Marks, *Precious Dust: The American Gold Rush Era, 1848–1900* (New York: William Morrow, 1994).

45   See Kathryn Morse, *The Nature of Gold: An Environmental History of the Klondike Gold Rush* (Seattle: Univ. of Washington Press, 2003), 16–39.

46   Frank L. Merrick, "The Alaska–Yukon–Pacific Exposition," *Alaska–Yukon Magazine* 2, no. 3 (September 1906), 2.

47   John Jasper Underwood, *Alaska: An Empire in the Making* (New York: Dodd, Mead and Co. 1913), 236.

48   Fridtjof Nansen, *Through Siberia: The Land of the Future*, trans. Arthur G. Chater (New York: Frederick A. Stokes, 1912), 350.

49   The seal is reproduced in Terrence Cole, "Promoting the Pacific Rim: The Alaska–Yukon–Pacific Exposition of 1909," *Alaska History* 6, no. 1 (Spring 1991): 19.

50   See Morgan Sherwood, "A North Pacific Bubble, 1902–1907," *Alaska History* 12, no. 1 (Spring 1997): 20.

51   James Wickersham, *Old Yukon: Tales, Trails, and Trials* (Washington, DC: Washington Law Book Co., 1938), 398 and 401. This theme pervades Davis, *Uncle Sam's Attic*.

52   See Harding's speech on Alaska printed in Archie W. Shiels, *Seward's Icebox: A Few Notes on the Development of Alaska, 1867–1932* (Seattle: 1933), 180.

53   Darwin quoted in Janet Browne, *Charles Darwin: The Power of Place* (New York: Alfred A. Knopf, 2002), 343.

54   Underwood, *Alaska: An Empire in the Making*, xiv, xvi.

55   J. A. Hellenthal, *The Alaskan Melodrama* (New York: Liveright, 1936), vii.

56   Jack Hines, *Minstrel of the North: An Alaskan Adventure* (New York: Greenberg, 1948), 98.

57   Wickersham, *Old Yukon*, 408.

58   Stephen Haycox, *Alaska: An American Colony* (Seattle: Univ. of Washington Press, 2002), 210.

59   *Skaguay News*, October 14, 1898; December 30, 1898.

60   Sam. C. Dunham, *The Goldsmith of Nome* (Washington, DC: Neale, 1901), 37.

61   Dunham, *Goldsmith of Nome*, v, 37, 39, 41, 50, 80.

62   See, for example, Lomen, *Fifty Years in Alaska*, 3–4.

63   William R. Hunt, *Distant Justice: Policing the Alaska Frontier* (Norman: Univ. of Oklahoma Press, 1987), 120, 127, 131, 135.

64   Records of the Alaska Territorial Legislature, 1913–1953, file M1012, roll 1, RG 38, National Archives and Records Administration, Anchorage.

65   In their extended and intelligent polemics against the federal government, two of American Alaska's early historians pointed to the graft and incompetence of government agents in Nome to support their anti–federal government sentiment. See Jeanette Paddock Nichols, *Alaska: A History of its Administration, Exploitation, and Industrial Development during its First Half Century Under the Rule of the United States* (Cleveland: Arthur H. Clark, 1924), 192–93. Here I am using this work as a primary source. Also see Ernest Gruening, *The State of Alaska: A Definitive History of America's Northernmost Frontier* (New York: Random House, 1968), 338.

66   Robert Fortuine, *Chills and Fever: Health and Disease in the Early History of Alaska* (Fairbanks: Univ. of Alaska Press, 1989), 177–78, 240.

67   Lyman L. Woodman, *Duty Station Northwest: The U.S. Army in Alaska and Western Canada, 1867–1987*, vol. 1 (Anchorage: Alaska Historical Society, 1996), 207.

68   Wickersham, *Old Yukon*, 410.

69   Hunt, *Distant Justice*, 84, 86, 92, 120, 123; Wickersham, *Old Yukon*, 408.

70   Hunt, *North of 53*, 253.

71   Adams, "Cape Nome Beach," 726.

72   See, for example, Madsen, *Arctic Trader*, 57.

73   Robert Alden Sterns, "The Morgan–Guggenheim Syndicate and the Development of Alaska, 1906–1915," PhD diss., University of California, Santa Barbara, 1967, 49–50.

74   Clark C. Spence, "The Ernst–Alaska Dredging Company: Small Dredge Technology on the Nome Beaches, 1910–1920," *Alaska History* 2, no. 1 (Winter 1986/87), 5.

75   Clark C. Spence, *The Northern Gold Fleet: Twentieth-Century Gold Dredging in Alaska* (Urbana: Univ. of Illinois Press, 1996), 31.

76   Unnamed source cited in Spence, *Northern Gold Fleet*, 70.

77   See Carl J. Lomen diaries, University of Alaska Fairbanks.

78   Ducker, "Gold-Rushers to the North," 5, 10.

79   Cited in Nichols, *Alaska*, 256.

80   Cole, "Promoting the Pacific Rim," 21.

81   Spence, *Northern Gold Fleet*, 59.

CHAPTER I: FORGING AMERICANNESS

1   William James, *The Principles of Psychology* (1890; repr., Cambridge, MA: Harvard Univ. Press, 1983), 279–80.

2   Ibid., 280–81.

3   Lanier McKee, *The Land of Nome* (New York: Grafton, 1902), 1; *Daily Alaskan*, July 8, 1899; and Frank Freidel, "Dissent in the Spanish-American War and the Philippine Insurrection," in *Dissent in Three American Wars*, ed. Samuel Eliot Morison and others (Cambridge, MA: Harvard Univ. Press, 1970). The tradition continues: "Nobody cares to read East Coast blowhards; let's hear from Alaskans," *Anchorage Daily News*, June 17, 2003.

4   James Ducker, "A Census Study of the Yukon and Alaskan Gold Rushes, 1896–1900," in *An Alaska Anthology: Interpreting the Past*, ed. Stephen W. Haycox and Mary Childers Mangusso, 208 (Seattle: Univ. of Washington Press, 1996).

5   Professionals—e.g., lawyers and doctors—composed about 8.5 percent of Nome's population in 1900, as compared to 2 percent of Skagway's population. About 17.4 percent of Nome's residents in Nome in 1900 were businessmen, as opposed to 10.6 percent in Skagway. Nearly 19 percent of Nomeites were employed in the food and drink business, as opposed to 5.5 percent in Skagway. Businessmen and restaurateurs had a vested interest in the promotion of stability. For census figures, see James H. Ducker, "Carmack's Alaskans: A Census Study of Alaskans in 1900," unpublished manuscript, 1983, 18. Also see Ducker, "A Census Study," 217.

6   See the photographs in Keith Wheeler, *The Alaskans* (Alexandria, VA: Time-Life Books, 1977), 158–59; Jane G. Haigh, *Alaska Pioneer Interiors* (Fairbanks: Tanana–Yukon Historical Society, 1986), 4–6; and see Louise L. Stevenson, *The Victorian Homefront: American Thought and Culture, 1860–1880* (Ithaca: Cornell Univ. Press, 1991), 1, 25.

7   For example, the following chapter titles: Lael Morgan, "Klondike Kate Rockwell: An Enduring Charmer" in *Good Time Girls of the Yukon Gold Rush* (Fairbanks: Epicenter, 1998); and Pierre Berton, "Being a Faithful Account of the Rise, Reign, and Violent Death of Jefferson 'Soapy' Smith, the Dictator of Skagway" in *The Klondike Fever: The Life and Death of the Last Gold Rush* (1958; repr., New York: Carroll and Graf, 2000). "The romantic stereotype of the frontier prostitute," writes Charlene Porsild, "almost never held true." See Porsild's *Gamblers and Dreamers: Women, Men and Community in the Klondike* (Vancouver: Univ. of British Columbia Press, 1998), 21. For an overview of the women who went to the Klondike gold rush, see Laurie Alberts, "Petticoats and Pickaxes," *Alaska Journal* (Summer 1977): 146–59.

8   E. S. Harrison, *Nome and Seward Peninsula: History, Description, Biographies and Stories* (Seattle: Metropolitan, 1905), 279, 280, 304.

9   Victoria Joan Moessner and Joanne E. Gates, *The Alaska–Klondike Diary of Elizabeth Robins, 1900* (Fairbanks: Univ. of Alaska Press, 1999), 19.

10 Kenneth J. Kutz, ed., *Nome Gold: Two Years of the Last Great Gold Rush in American History, 1900–1902* (Darien, CT: Gold Fever Publishing, 1991), 78.

11 *Nome News*, June 23, 1903.

12 Of course, since James's time professional psychologists and psychiatrists have amassed a vast literature on the "self." Background works I read in preparation for this study are Dan P. McAdams, *The Stories We Live By: Personal Myths and the Making of the Self* (New York: Guilford, 1993); and Arnold M. Ludwig, *How Do We Know Who We Are?: A Biography of the Self* (Oxford: Oxford Univ. Press, 1997).

13 Kutz, *Nome Gold*, 27; and L. H. French, *Nome Nuggets* (1905; repr., Anchorage: Alaska Northwest, 1983), 43.

14 Kutz, *Nome Gold*, 27.

15 See the correspondence December 10, 1900–February 15, 1901, Interior Department Territorial Papers: Alaska, 1869–1911, file M430, roll 7.

16 Ibid., 26, 29, and 38.

17 McKee, *Land of Nome*, 30, 31, 33, and 41.

18 See, for example, *Nome Gold Digger,* May 11, 1904.

19 See Carrie M. McLain, *Gold-Rush Nome* (Portland, OR: Graphic Arts Center, 1969), 7, 35 (photograph).

20 *Nome Gold Digger*, April 11, 1900; Kutz, *Nome Gold*, 26; and French, *Nome Nuggets*, 11.

21 See Kathleen Dalton, *Theodore Roosevelt: A Strenuous Life* (New York: Knopf, 2002).

22 James, *Principles of Psychology*, 280.

23 William J. Murtagh, "Some Homes of Nome," *Alaska Journal* 4, no. 1 (Winter 1974): 17–20. A large percentage, perhaps more than a third, of Nome's residents were foreign-born. But some three-fourths of them had become citizens of the United States before going to Nome. See Ducker, "Gold-Rushers to the North," 5.

24 See, for example, the *Nome Gold Digger,* February 14, 1900.

25 Stefansson, *Discovery*, 115, and Mitchell, *Sold American*, 144–49. Also see James H. Ducker, "Out of Harm's Way: Relocating Northwest Alaska Eskimos, 1907–1917," *Indian Culture and Research Journal* 20, no. 1 (1996): 43–64.

26 See, for example, French, *Nome Nuggets*, 35; Moessner and Gates, *Alaska–Klondike Diary*, 317; Leroy S. Townsend, *The Alaska Gold Rush Letters and Photographs of Leroy S. Townsend, 1898–1899*, 93; Vilhjalmur Stefansson, *My Life with the Eskimo* (1913; repr., New York: Collier Books, 1966), 71; and Haycox, *Alaska: An American Colony*, 209–10.

27 *Nome Gold Digger*, February 7, 1900; February 28, 1900. Also see the *Nome News*, April 17, 1903. The Nelson Act of 1905 provided for schools where white and "mixed-blood" students would learn together. See Ronald Lautaret, ed., *Alaskan Historical Documents since 1867* (Jefferson, NC: Mcfarland & Company, 1989), 51.

28 Moessner and Gates, *Alaska–Klondike Diary*, 330; Eleanor Ransom Mayhew and Ellsworth Luce West, *Captain's Papers* (Barre, MA: Barre Publishing Co., 1965), 84; Frank L. Shrader and Alfred H. Brooks, *Preliminary Report on the Cape Nome Gold Region* (Washington, DC: Government Printing Office, 1900), 46. Also see Terrence Cole, "A History of the Nome Gold Rush: The Poor Man's Paradise" (PhD diss., University of Washington, 1983), 47; and, on lawyers in the Klondike, Porsild, *Gamblers and Dreamers*, 164–67.

29 For example, *Nome Gold Digger*, December 6, 1899, and *Nome News*, May 8, 1903.

30 See, for example, John F. Stacey, *To Alaska for Gold* (n.p., n.p., c. 1906 [repr., Fairfield, WA: Ye Galleon Press, 1973]), 69; and Jeff Kunkel, ed., *Alaska Gold: Life on the New Frontier, 1898–1906* (San Francisco: Scotwall Associates, 1997), 92, 146.

31 See Fred Lockley, *History of the First Free Delivery Service of Mail in Alaska at Nome, Alaska in 1900* (Seattle: Shorey Book Store, 1900); Kutz, *Nome Gold*, passim; and Kunkel, *Alaska Gold*, 59.

32 On the drive to establish a "respectable" society, see Morgan, *Good Time Girls*. Also see *Nome Gold Digger*, November 15, 1899; Kutz, *Nome Gold*, 113; and Stevenson, *The Victorian Homefront*, 15. Also see the satirical cartoons in *Arctic Weekly Sun*, July 15, 1900; and *Arctic Midnight Sun*, August 5, 1900.

33 Kunkel, *Alaska Gold*, 85.

34 William J. Murtagh, "Some Homes of Nome," *Alaska Journal* 4, no. 1 (Winter 1974): 20; Moessner and Gates, *Alaska–Klondike Diary*, 53; and see Christopher Benfey, *The Great Wave: Gilded Age Misfits, Japanese Eccentrics, and the Opening of Old Japan* (New York: Random House, 2003).

35 Thomas J. Schlereth, *Victorian America: Transformations in Everyday Life, 1876–1915* (New York: HarperPerennial, 1991), 221; Pierre Berton, *The Klondike Fever: The Life and Death of the Last Gold Rush* (New York: Carroll and Graf, 1958 [repr., 2000]), 128–29; Terrence Cole, *Wheels on Ice: Bicycling in Alaska, 1898–1908* (Anchorage: Alaska Northwest, n.d.), 9–20; and Kutz, *Nome Gold*, 141.

36 Reed, *Boyhood in the Nome Gold Camp*, 52.

37 Evangeline Atwood, *Frontier Politics: Alaska's James Wickersham* (Portland, OR: Binford and Mort, 1979), 87.

38 *Nome Gold Digger*, May 11, 1904; May 9, 1900; *Nome News*, September 15, 1900; and see the photographs in Terrence Cole, *Nome: "City of Golden Beaches"* (Anchorage: Alaska Geographic Society, 1984), 42, 64, 68, and 69. My emphasis. To be sure, there were institutions that emphasized Nome's geographic location, e.g., the Arctic Saloon and Northern Saloon.

39 Shrader and Brooks, *Preliminary Report*, 46. Also see, for another example, *Nome Gold Digger*, January 17, 1900.

40 *Nome Gold Digger*, January 3, 1900. In 1900 the popular Reverend Russell H. Conwell said in some 6,000 lectures that "You should be a righteous man. If you were, you would be rich." Conwell's famous lecture is excerpted in David M. Kennedy and Thomas A. Bailey, *The American Spirit*, vol. 2 (Boston: Houghton Mifflin Company, 2006), 76.

41 Alice Palmer Henderson, *The Rainbow's End: Alaska* (New York: Herbert S. Stone, 1898), dedication page; James R. Shortridge, "American Perceptions of the Agricultural Potential of Alaska, 1867–1958" (PhD diss., University of Kansas, 1972), 103; and Arrell Morgan Gibson, *Yankees in Paradise: The Pacific Basin Frontier* (Albuquerque: Univ. of New Mexico Press, 1993), 343. For the biblical allusions see James 2:18–26 and Rev. 22:5.

42 See the photographs in Cole, *Nome*, 27, 67. Also see the photographs in Mayhew and West, *Captain's Papers*, between pp. 104 and 105; and in Kunkel, *Alaska Gold*, 45–46.

43 McKee, *Land of Nome*, 52. McKee indicates that he saw this near the Fourth of July, but it seems likely that the flag was placed on the tent before then. Also see Moessner and Gates, *Alaska–Klondike Diary*, 70, 133; and Kutz, *Nome Gold*, 65.

44 See the photograph in Wheeler, *The Alaskans*, 170.

45 Harrison, *Nome and Seward Peninsula*, 91.

46 See the photograph in Cole, *Nome*, 42; and Richard P. Emanuel, *The Golden Gamble* (Anchorage: Alaska Geographic, 1997), 61.

47 I examined numerous photographs in Stan Cohen, *Gold Rush Gateway: Skagway and Dyea, Alaska* (Missoula: Pictorial Histories, 1986), 2, 3, 15, 19, 22, 33, 34, 36, 37; and Howard Clifford, *The Skagway Story* (Anchorage: Alaska Northwest, 1975), 76, 79.

48 Americans who recall the sudden appearance of myriad American flags after the terrorist attacks on the World Trade Center and Pentagon on September 11, 2001, understand the soothing symbolism of flag waving. When Robert E. Lee took his Confederate forces into

Pennsylvania in the summer of 1863, Yankee townspeople responded by hoisting numerous Union flags. And during combat, an inordinate amount of blood and energy was spent protecting and capturing flags. See Stephen W. Sears, *Gettysburg* (New York: Houghton Mifflin, 2003), 146, 207, 211, 218, 221, 223, 248, 304.

49   Stefansson, *Adventure of Wrangel Island*, 120.

50   Quoted in Frederick Merk, *Manifest Destiny and Mission in American History* (Cambridge, MA: Harvard Univ. Press, 1963 [repr., 1995]), 232.

51   *Nome Daily Gold Digger*, November 24, 1906; November 30, 1906; August 15, 1906. "[T]he theater became a setting for spoofing, stereotyping, and sympathizing with the Irish, Italians, Germans and Jews, as well as blacks and 'rubes' fresh from the countryside." Schlereth, *Victorian America*, 232.

52   Carl J. Lomen diaries, May 11, 1900; Loyal Wirt, *Alaskan Adventures* (New York: Fleming H. Revell Co., 1937), 55; *Aurora*, 1910, 5–8, 29; Louise Anita Martin, *North to Nome* (Chicago: Whitman, 1939), 289; Charles Madsen, *Arctic Trader* (New York: Dodd, Mead, 1957), 68; Ruthmary McDowell Papers, Box 1, folders 28 and 32, University of Alaska Fairbanks. This paragraph borrows from Preston Jones, "Yankees in Parkas, 53.

53   *Nome Daily Gold Digger*, December 11, 1906.

54   Ibid., February 5, 1905.

55   Ibid., July 21, 1906.

56   William Bruce Wheeler and Susan D. Becker, eds., *Discovering the American Past: A Look at the Evidence*, vol. 2 (Boston: Houghton Mifflin, 2002), 68, 73; and *Nome Daily Gold Digger*, January 15, 1907.

57   *Nome Daily Gold Digger*, January 24, 1907.

58   Ibid., November 29, 1906; December 10, 1906.

59   Ibid., January 4, 1907; June 29, 1907.

60   Winthrop Talbot, ed., *Americanization: Principles of Americanism, Essentials of Americanization, Technic* [sic] *of Race-Assimilation* (New York: Wilson, 1917), 50; *Nome Daily Gold Digger*, June 28, 1907. Emphasis in the original.

61   Talbot, *Americanization*, 42; *Nome Daily Gold Digger*, October 29, 1906.

62   *Nome Daily Gold Digger*, February 1, 1906; January 29, 1907.

63   Ibid., February 1, 1906.

64   Ella Higginson, *Alaska: The Great Country* (New York: Macmillan, 1908), 516–19. Also see a comparable 1905 article, "The Development of Nome," discussed in Walter R. Borneman, *Alaska: Saga of a Bold Land* (New York: HarperCollins, 2003), 212.

65   *Nome Daily Gold Digger*, March 11, 1903.

66   Ibid., October 26, 1906.

67   Nichols, *Alaska*, 211.

CHAPTER 2: REACHING FOR EMPIRE

1   Quoted in Merk, *Manifest Destiny*, 29.

2   Stephen Haycox, *Frigid Embrace: Politics, Economics and Environment in Alaska* (Corvallis: Oregon State Univ. Press, 2002), ix.

3   *Council City News*, January 20, 1906.

4   This is one theme of John Winthrop's highly influential sermon, "Modell of Christian Charity" (1630). Similar ideas pervade the documents included in Conrad Cherry, ed., *God's New Israel: Religious Interpretations of American Destiny* (Chapel Hill: Univ. of North Carolina Press, 1998).

5   O'Sullivan quoted in Anders Stephanson, *Manifest Destiny: American Expansionism and the Empire of Right* (New York: Hill and Wang, 1995), xi.

6   *Nome Daily Gold Digger*, December 1, 1906; Charles R. Tuttle, *Alaska: Its Meaning to the World, Its Resources, Its Opportunities* (Seattle: Franklin Shuey, 1914), 295–96.

7   See, for example, the *Nome News*, April 17, 1903, and June 30, 1903; and Shortridge, "American Perceptions," 86.

8   *Nome Daily Gold Digger*, December 1, 1906.

9   Ducker, "A Census Study," 212.

10   *Fort Wrangel News*, July 20, 1898.

11   See Doug Owram, *The Promise of Eden: The Canadian Expansionist Movement and the Idea of the West, 1865–1900* (Toronto: Univ. of Toronto Press, 1992); and Robert Hill, *Voice of the Vanishing Minority: Robert Sellar and the Huntington Gleaner, 1863–1919* (Montreal-Kingston: McGill-Queen's Univ. Press, 1999).

12   See, for example, Gen. 1:26–28.

13   By the mid-1840s, some manifest destinarians included "the icy wilderness of the North" in their visions of America's future continental empire. See Merk, *Manifest Destiny*, 46.

14   Quoted in Ted C. Hinckley, *The Americanization of Alaska, 1867–1897* (Palo Alto: Pacific Books, 1972), 144.

15   *Alaska Free Press*, January 15, 1887.

16   *Skaguay News*, July 1, 1898.

17   *Nome News*, August 14, 1903; and French, *Nome Nuggets*, 43.

18   See *Le Journal du Madawaska*, August 19, 1903, 3.

19   Cole, "History of the Nome Gold Rush," 9; and Mayhew and West, *Captain's Papers*, 96.

20   Hinckley, *Americanization of Alaska*, 20.

21   *Alaska Free Press* (Juneau), January 15, 1887.

22   McKee, *Land of Nome*, 2.

23   Cited in the *Nome Gold Digger*, April 18, 1900.

24   Quoted in Cole, *Nome*, 9.

25   *Nome Gold Digger*, November 8, 1899.

26   Ibid., November 7, 1900.

27   As one Canadian nationalist song put it: "Oh, we are men of the Northern Zone/ Shall a bit be placed in our mouth?/ If ever a Northman lost his throne/ Did the conqueror come from the South?/ Nay, nay—and the answer blent/ In chorus is southward sent/ Since when has a Southern's conquering steel/ Hewed out in North a throne?/ Since when has a Southerner placed his heel/ On the men of the Northern Zone?" Robert Kernigan, "The Men of the Northern Zone," in George W. Ross, ed., *Patriotic Recitations and Arbor Day Exercises* (Toronto: Warwick Brothers and Rutter, 1893), 64. Also see Vilhjalmur Stefansson, *The Northward Course of Empire* (New York: Macmillan, 1924), 84; and Merk, *Manifest Destiny*, 240.

28   Lockley, *History of the First Free Delivery Service*, 1.

29   *Nome Daily Gold Digger*, December 1, 1906; October 23, 1907.

30   See, for example, Sherry Simpson, *The Way Winter Comes: Alaska Stories* (Seattle: Sasquatch Books, 1998).

31   The classic document, "The Providential Mission of the French Canadians," is excerpted in Ramsay Cook, ed., *French Canadian Nationalism: An Anthology* (Toronto: Macmillan of Canada, 1969), 92–106.

32   See, for example, J. Castell Hopkins, *Progress of Canada in the Century* (Toronto: Linscott, 1902); and F. A. Wightman, *Our Canadian Heritage, Its Resources and Possibilities* (Toronto: William Briggs, 1905).

33   See, for example, David Traxel, "War Fever," in *1898: The Birth of the American Century* (New York: Vintage Books, 1998).

34   *Daily Alaskan*, February 28, 1898; May 4, 1899. Also see *Skaguay News*, July 1, 1898; October 29, 1897.

35   *The Dyea Trail*, April 2, 1898.

36   *Teller News*, April 11, 1901.

37   *Nome News*, September 15, 1900; *Nome Gold Digger*, March 14, 1900.

38   *Nome Gold Digger*, January 24, 1900.

39   Ibid., November 20, 1899; February 28, 1900; March 28, 1900.

40   George Brown Tindall and David Emory Shi, *America: A Narrative History* (New York: W. W. Norton and Co., 1999), 1029.

41   Shrader and Brooks, *Preliminary Report*, 45–46. Also see Moessner and Gates, *Alaska–Klondike Diary*, 317–18.

42   M. Clark, *Roadhouse Tales; or, Nome in 1900* (Girard, KS: Appeal Publishing, 1902), 32; and *Nome Gold Digger*, May 2, 1900.

43   See, for example, Marian M. George, ed., *Little Journeys to Alaska and Canada* (Chicago: A. Flanagan, 1901), 3, 11.

44   Walter LaFeber, *The New Empire: An Interpretation of American Expansionism, 1860–1898* (Ithaca: Cornell Univ. Press, 1967), 409; Jean Heffer, *The United States and the Pacific: History of a Frontier*, trans. W. Donald Wilson (South Bend, IN: Univ. of Notre Dame Press, 2002), 96.

45   *Alaska Journal*, April 22, 1893.

46   Mckee, *Land of Nome*, 24.

47   *Skaguay News*, February 24, 1899.

48   *Alaska Miner*, February 3, 1900; and Morgan B. Sherwood, *Exploration of Alaska, 1865–1900* (New Haven: Yale Univ. Press, 1965), 15.

49   *Alaska Miner*, January 13, 1900.

50   *Nome Gold Digger*, March 14, 1900.

51   *Daily Alaskan*, July 25, 1898.

52   *Nome Nugget*, June 13, 1903.

53   LaFeber, *New Empire*, 300–11; and *Nome Gold Digger*, March 28, 1900.

54   Reynolds–Alaska Company Prospectus and E. A. Hitchcock to John G. Brady, March 6, 1905, Interior Department Alaska file, roll 11.

55   *Nome News*, June 16, 1903. My italics.

56   A "Seattle paper" quoted at length in the *Nome News*, June 19, 1903.

57   Joseph F. Evans to Secretary of the Treasury, November 12, 1900, Interior Department Alaska file, roll 13. In a similar vein, Vilhjalmur Stefansson wrote that "[w]henever the Arctic shall become as crossable to us as the Mediterranean was to the Phoenicians, it will become more of a connecting link between the continents than a barrier." In *Adventure of Wrangel Island*, 69.

58   Joseph F. Evans to Secretary of the Treasury, November 12, 1900, Interior Department Alaska file, roll 13.

59   Franklin Ward Burch, "Alaska's Railroad Frontier: Railroads and Federal Development Policy, 1898–1915" (PhD diss., Catholic University of America, 1965), 147–48. Also see Tuttle, *Alaska*, 296–99.

60   *Nome Gold Digger*, February 28, 1900.

61   Ibid., August 1, 1900.

62   *Alaska Free Press*, July 19, 1890; see Deut. 34:4.

63 *Nome Gold Digger*, December 27, 1899; May 30, 1900. For an overview of thinking in the nineteenth and twentieth centuries about a bridge across the Bering Strait, see Terrence Cole, "The Bridge to Tomorrow: Visions of the Bering Strait Bridge," *Alaska History* 5, no. 2 (Fall 1990): 1–15.

64 Mayhew and West, *Captain's Papers*, 136; and William R. Hunt, *Arctic Passage: The Turbulent History of the Land and People of the Bering Sea, 1867–1975* (New York: Scribner, 1975), 209–10.

65 Mayhew and West, *Captain's Papers*, 97–99, 123–24; Dan Gallagher, *Florida's Great Ocean Railway: Building the Key West Extension* (Sarasota, FL: Pineapple Press, 2003); and *Le Journal du Madawaska*, September 2, 1903.

66 *Nome Daily Gold Digger*, October 23, 1907.

67 Ibid., April 4, 1900; May 23, 1900.

68 *Skaguay News*, July 15, 1898. Also see the *Daily Alaskan*, March 16, 1900.

69 See Gerald O. Williams, *The Bering Sea Fur Seal Dispute, 1885–1911* (Juneau: Alaska Maritime Publications, 1984); Gerald O. Williams, "Michael J. Healy and the Alaska Maritime Frontier, 1880–1902" (PhD diss., University of Oregon, 1987); Joan Antonson Mohr, "Alaska and the Sea: A Survey of Alaska's Maritime History" (Anchorage: Office of History and Archaeology, 1979), 48–71; and, on navy activity in the Pacific generally, Gibson, *Yankees in Paradise*, 313–45.

70 *Teller News*, March 28, 1901; *Nome Daily Gold Digger*, June 24, 1907.

71 One could say that this trend began with the failure of the Russian-American telegraph in 1867. See Rosemary Neering, *Continental Dash: The Russian-American Telegraph* (Gouges, BC: Horsdal and Schubart, 1989).

72 Cole, "History of the Nome Gold Rush," 233; and Heffer, *United States and the Pacific*, 210.

73 See Hunt, *Arctic Passage*, 214–15.

74 Joseph F. Evans to Secretary of the Treasury, November 12, 1900, Interior Department Alaska file, roll 13; and Shrader and Brooks, *Preliminary Report*, 39.

75 Burch, "Alaska's Railroad Frontier," 87.

76 Howard Clifford, *Rails North: The Railroads of Alaska and the Yukon* (Seattle: Superior Publishing Company, 1981), 169–77. Also see Burch, "Alaska's Railroad Frontier," 84–89 and 186–87.

77 *Nome Daily Gold Digger*, January 31, 1907.

78 Ibid., November 24, 1906; January 4, 1907.

79 Walter McDougall, *Let the Sea Make a Noise: A History of the North Pacific from Magellan to MacArthur* (New York: Basic Books, 1993), 419.

80 Brady to Secretary of the Interior, January 19, 1905; and Secretary of the Navy to Secretary of the Interior, January 25, 1905, Interior Department Alaska file, roll 11.

81 See Report of the Secretary of War, 43–44, in Interior Department Alaska file, roll 11.

82 Evans quoted in *Nome Gold Digger*, May 30, 1900.

83 Evans to Secretary of the Treasury, May 1, 1900, Interior Department Alaska file, roll 13.

84 Evans to Secretary of the Treasury, November 12, 1900; and D. H. Jarvis to Secretary of the Treasury, October 6, 1900, Interior Department Alaska file, roll 13.

85 Shrader and Brooks, *Preliminary Report*, 45.

86 Jarvis to Secretary of the Treasury, March 16, 1901, Interior Department Alaska file, roll 14.

87 See Evans's employee evaluations, December 2, 1901, Interior Department Alaska file, roll 14.

88 Evans to Secretary of the Treasury, December 6, 1901, Interior Department Alaska file, roll 14.

89 San Francisco Chamber of Commerce to Secretary of the Treasury, c. May 17, 1900, Interior Department Alaska file, roll 13.

90 Shartzer to Secretary of the Treasury, April 2, 1900; Evans to J. C. McCook, July 19, 1900; Evans to Secretary of the Treasury, November 15, 1900, Interior Department Alaska file, roll 13; and Supervising Special Agent to Jarvis, March 19, 1901, Interior Department Alaska file, roll 14.

91 Parker to D. B. Henderson, April 12, 1900, Interior Department Alaska file, roll 13.

92 Evans to Secretary of the Treasury, May 5, 1900, Interior Department Alaska file, roll 13.

93 In the fall of 2001 a single part-time agent in Nome represented U.S. Customs and the Immigration and Naturalization Services, which have since been absorbed by the Department of Homeland Security. In 2001, the U.S. government moved to close the port at Nome, although this move was "thwarted." See: http://nugget.nomenugget.com/20011101/local.html.

94 Evans to Secretary of the Treasury, May 1, 1900, Interior Department Alaska file, roll 13.

95 *Nome Gold Digger*, May 30, 1900.

96 In 1905, the permanency of Nome was still questioned by the federal government. See *Nome News*, April 14, 1905.

97 Shrader and Brooks, *Preliminary Report*, 48.

98 *Nome Nugget*, April 20, 1903.

99 *Nome News*, July 3, 1903.

100 Ibid., August 14, 1903. My emphases.

101 See Benson Lee Grayson, "Lost Opportunity: The Alaska–Siberia Tunnel," *Asian Affairs* 64, no. 1 (1977): 66.

102 Herman Rosenthal, "From New York to Paris by Rail," *Review of Reviews,* May 1906, 592.

103 "Drawing Board," *U.S. News and World Report*, July 30–June 7, 2003, 42.

104 Howard Clifford, *Rails North*, 181. In "Lost Opportunity," Grayson calls the tunnel scheme a "serious proposal" and even lays the Russian Revolution at the feet of those who failed to get it done. "The shortages and disorder caused by the lack of rail transportation brought about the revolution of February 1917," he writes (68). But, the argument goes, if the tunnel had been built, there would have been no shortages, no Bolshevik Revolution, hence no communist Russia and no Cold War. Since small-time railroads on the Seward Peninsula could not survive, and since plans to connect Nome to the Outside were deemed impractical, it is hard to see how this tunnel scheme could have been "serious" in any sense except in the minds of a few investors and big project schemers.

105 *Nome News*, July 7, 1905.

106 *Nome Daily Gold Digger*, October 4, 1970.

107 "Report from the Chief of Engineers on Preliminary Examination and Survey of Nome Harbor, Alaska," House of Representatives, 71st Congress, 2nd session, document 404, 2.

108 *Nome Gold Digger*, December 31, 1902.

109 See Spence, *Northern Gold Fleet*, 13–55.

110 See the introduction to chapter 1.

111 *Nome Nugget*, July 1, 1905; *Council News*, April 21, 1906.

112 *Nome Nugget*, July 1, 1905.

113 As former *Anchorage Daily News* columnist Mike Doogan told me, part of enduring Alaskan mythology is the belief that "you have to be a special kind of person to live here" (interview with the author, June 10, 2003). This sense of differentness pervades books written by Alaskans, such as Julia Scully, *Outside Passage: A Memoir of an Alaskan Childhood* (New York: Random House, 1999); Norma Cobb and Charles Sasser, *Arctic Homestead: The True Story of One Family's Survival and Courage in the Alaskan Wilds* (New York: St. Martin's, 2003); and

Simpson, *Way Winter Comes*. Also see Lee J. Cuba, *Identity and Community on the Alaskan Frontier* (Philadelphia: Temple Univ. Press, 1987), 92–117.

114 See, for example, *Daily Alaskan*, March 9, 1900; *Nome Gold Digger*, January 1, 1902; McKee, *Nome Gold*, 258.

115 See, for example, Secretary of War to Secretary of the Interior, July 12, 1900, Interior Department Alaska file, roll 7. Also see the citations of microfilmed government documents in the pages above and below. And see Haycox, *Alaska: An American Colony*, 210–18.

116 *Nome Nugget*, January 18, 1903; March 28, 1903.

117 *Daily Alaskan*, January 1, 1900. In the early twenty-first century, secession remained a live if very minor political topic of discussion. See, for example, the cartoon in the *Anchorage Daily News*, June 29, 2003, sec. H.

118 *Nome Nugget*, June 24, 1905.

119 Ibid.

120 *Nome News*, May 18, 1902.

121 *Nome Nugget*, June 24, 1905. Also see *Nome Nugget*, July 1, 1905.

122 *Nome Daily Gold Digger*, January 31, 1907; *Council News*, December 22, 1906.

123 In 1910 the population of St. Michael village stood at 415, and the district of Port Clarence, which included several villages, stood at 1,007. See Alden M. Rollins, ed., "Census Alaska: Numbers of Inhabitants, 1792–1970" (1978), unpublished manuscript, held at Alaska Resources Library and Information Services, Anchorage.

CHAPTER 3: WINNING

1   George S. Gibbs, "Transportation Methods in Alaska," *National Geographic Magazine* 17, no. 2 (February 1906): 76.

2   Harrison, *Nome and Seward Peninsula*, 179.

3   *Nome Pioneer Press*, September 8, 1908.

4   See Karl Meyer and Shareen Brysac, "The Russians Are Coming," in *Tournament of Shadows: The Great Game and the Race for Empire in Asia* (London: Abacus, 1999).

5   *Council City News*, November 11, 1905; April 14, 1906; *Nome Semi-Weekly Nugget*, April 13, 1904.

6   See the correspondence between John Brady and the Department of the Interior, May 18, 1905–July 13, 1905. Interior Department Alaska file, roll 12.

7   On Canada, see Robert Craig Brown and Ramsay Cook, *Canada, 1896–1921: A Nation Transformed* (Toronto: McClelland and Stewart, 1991), 68–70.

8   *Council City News*, December 22, 1906; *Nome Daily Gold Digger*, October 22, 1907; *Nome Tri-Weekly Nugget*, February 5, 1907; *Nome Daily Nugget*, June 12, 1907; June 18, 1907.

9   *Nome Daily Gold Digger*, November 16, 1907. This came eleven months after the *Gold Digger* had decried American prejudice against Japan and the Japanese (January 4, 1907).

10 Lloyd C. Griscom to John Hay, April 5, 1905, Interior Department Alaska file, roll 12.

11 *Nome Daily Nugget*, June 12, 1907.

12 Goetze Collection, vol. 2, photograph number B01.41.181, AMHA.

13 *Council City News*, December 16, 1906. Rudyard Kipling's "White Man's Burden" was published in the American magazine *McClure's* in February 1899.

14 *Nome Daily Gold Digger*, October 31, 1906.

15 For an example of a common view of the races in the early twentieth century, see "Types and Development of Man" (1904) in William Bruce Wheeler and Susan D. Becker, eds., *Discovering the American Past: A Look at the Evidence*, vol. 2 (New York: Houghton Mifflin, 1998), 115.

16 Harrison, *Nome and Seward Peninsula*, 183–84.

17 Ibid., 158–60.

18 Alice Osborne, "The Council City and Solomon River Railroad," *Alaska Journal* 5, no. 1 (Winter 1975): 50, 52.

19 Paul Johnson, *A History of the American People* (San Francisco: HarperPerennial, 1999), 564.

20 Harrison, *Nome and Seward Peninsula*, 183.

21 Ibid., 205.

22 Ibid., 274.

23 Ibid., 183.

24 See, for example, *Council News*, December 22, 1906.

25 *Nome Daily Gold Digger*, January 2, 1908.

26 *Nome Tri-Weekly Nugget*, June 12, 1907.

27 *Nome Daily Gold Digger*, January 10, 1906.

28 *Nome Daily Nugget*, June 12, 1907.

29 *Nome Daily Gold Digger*, August 10, 1906; August 11, 1906; August 13, 1906.

30 *Nome Industrial Worker*, August 9, 1908.

31 *Nome Daily Gold Digger*, October 6, 1906; October 30, 1906.

32 *Nome Daily Nugget*, June 15, 1907.

33 *Nome Daily Gold Digger*, October 7, 1907.

34 Wilford B. Hoggatt to Secretary of the Interior, August 20, 1906, Interior Department Alaska file, roll 15; Harrison, *Nome and Seward Peninsula*, 161; *Nome Daily Nugget*, June 17, 1907.

35 *Council News*, April 21, 1906.

36 *Council City News*, March 17, 1906; February 3, 1906; *Nome Daily Gold Digger*, November 30, 1906; October 4, 1907.

37 See the report of Revenue Cutter Service First Lieutenant D. H. Jarvis, c. January 1905, Interior Department Alaska file, roll 11.

38 Harrison, *Nome and Seward Peninsula*, 143.

39 U.S. Acting Attorney General to George Borchsenius, August 1, 1903ff, Interior Department Alaska file, roll 9.

40 *Nome Daily Gold Digger*, August 15, 1906.

41 *Council News*, December 2, 1906.

42 See chapter 2.

43 *Council City News*, February 3, 1906; November 4, 1905.

44 *Council News*, April 28, 1906; Krug and Krug, *One Dog Short*, 86.

45 *Council City News*, December 30, 1905.

46 *Council City News*, April 6, 1906.

47 *Nome Daily Gold Digger*, December 28, 1906.

48 See "Alaska Newspapers on microfilm, 1866–1998" at: http://www.library.state.ak.us/hist/newspaper/news.html.

49 *Nome Daily Gold Digger*, December 14, 1906.

50 *Council City News*, December 2, 1905; *Nome Daily Gold Digger*, December 14, 1906.

51 *Council City News*, December 30, 1905; Harrison, *Nome and Seward Peninsula*, 157.

52 *Council City News*, December 30, 1905.

53 See the example of E. B. O'Connor's correspondence, December 29, 1905—August 12, 1906, Interior Department Alaska file, roll 14; *Council City News*, December 2, 1905.

54 *Council City News*, February 17, 1906; March 17, 1906; April 14, 1906; April 21, 1906; December 22, 1906.

55　　Osborne, "Council City," 53.

56　　*Council City News*, December 30, 1905; *Council News*, January 5, 1907.

57　　*Council News*, January 5, 1907.

58　　See, for example, the changes of address on the correspondence related to E. B. O'Connor, December 29, 1905–August 12, 1906, Interior Department Alaska file, roll 14.

59　　Ibid.

60　　*Nome Daily Nugget*, June 22, 1912.

61　　N. H. Castle, "A Short History of Council and Cheenik," *The Alaska Pioneer* 1, no. 1 (June 1912): 8–14.

62　　Rickard, *Through the Yukon and Alaska*, 368 and 372.

63　　Sally Carrigher, *Moonlight at Midday* (New York: Knopf, 1959); Donald J. Orth, *Dictionary of Alaska Place Names* (Washington, DC: Government Printing Office, 1971), 241. I base my claim about population in the early twenty-first century on conversations with people living on the Seward Peninsula in the summer of 2004.

64　　Orth, *Dictionary of Alaska Place Names*, 694, 955.

65　　*Nome Daily Nugget*, October 21, 1909.

66　　Taft cited in *Nome Daily Nugget*, October 21, 1909, 1.

67　　L. D. Kitchener, *Flag over the North* (Seattle: Superior Publishing, 1954), 252–53.

68　　Harrison, *Nome and Seward Peninsula*, 202, 204, 206, 212, 217, 221, 241, 247, 249, 255.

69　　*Nome Daily Nugget*, June 18, 1907.

70　　Ibid., June 12, 1907.

71　　*Nome Pioneer Press*, November 14, 1907; November 21, 1907; August 17, 1908.

72　　Ibid., August 17, 1908.

73　　Harrison, *Nome and Seward Peninsula*, 240, 246, 250.

74　　Ibid., 167–68.

75　　*Nome Daily Gold Digger*, July 28, 1906; October 24, 1906; January 15, 1907. My italics.

76　　Ibid., June 28, 1907.

77　　Ibid., November 12, 1906.

78　　Ibid., June 21, 1907.

79　　Harrison, *Nome and Seward Peninsula*, 56; *Nome Pioneer Weekly News*, May 12, 1905.

80　　*Nome Pioneer Press*, November 23, 1907; Glenda Choate and Thomas Harrison, "Chief Boatswain Thomas Austin Ross and the U.S. Life Saving Station, Nome, Alaska, 1905–1935," unpublished paper held at Anchorage Municipal Public Library, 6; Krug and Krug, *One Dog Short*, 90, 122.

81　　*Nome Weekly Nugget*, June 19, 1909.

82　　*Nome Daily Gold Digger*, October 27, 1906.

83　　Terrence Cole, "Baseball Above and Below Zero: The National Pastime in Alaska," *Alaska Journal* 13, no. 3 (Summer 1983): 130, 135.

84　　Norm Bolotin, "Nome's 1907 Version of the Globetrotters," *Alaska Journal* 9, no. 4 (Autumn 1979): 67.

85　　Spence, *Northern Gold Fleet*, 29.

86　　James C. Foster, "AFL, IWW and Nome: 1905–1908," *Alaska Journal* 5, no. 2 (Spring 1975): 66–73.

87　　U.S. Geological Survey to Secretary of the Interior, March 29, 1905, Interior Department Alaska file, roll 12.

88　　*Nome Daily Gold Digger*, May 18, 1904; June 24, 1907.

89　　Ibid., October 20, 1906.

90   *Nome Daily Nugget,* June 17, 1907.

91   Hunt, *North of 53,* 225.

92   Bankruptcy Case Files of the U.S. District Court for District and Territory of Alaska, Second Division, 1901–1953, National Archives and Records Administration, Anchorage, file M1966, roll 1 (case 21).

93   Harrison, *Nome and Seward Peninsula,* 58, 72, 74, 76; *Nome Pioneer Press,* November 23, 1907; December 21, 1907.

94   Admiralty Case Files of the U.S. District Court for the District and Territory of Alaska, Second Division, 1899–1950, National Archives and Records Administration, Anchorage, file M1967, roll 11 (cases 103A and 106A).

95   *Nome Semi-Weekly News,* September 15, 1905.

96   John Poling, "A History of the Nome, Alaska, Public Schools: 1899–1958" (master's thesis, University of Alaska, 1970). Also available online at http://www.alaskool.org/native_ed/PolingNPS/CHIV.htm.

97   *Nome Daily Gold Digger,* October 7, 1907.

98   Alfred H. Brooks and others, *Mineral Resources in Alaska, 1916* (Washington, DC: Government Printing Office, 1918), 456.

99   *Nome Daily Nugget,* August 1, 1907.

100 Poling, "History of the Nome, Alaska, Public Schools."

101 *Nome Daily Gold Digger,* July 21, 1906.

102 Ibid., October 24, 1906.

103 Ibid., December 14, 1906.

104 Ibid., December 18, 1906.

CHAPTER 4: COMMUNITY

1   *In hoc signo vinces,* "By this sign you shall conquer," what the Roman emperor Constantine was supposed to have heard from the heavens before a battle. The sign was a Christian cross.

2   Hugh Brogan, *The Penguin History of the USA* (New York: Penguin, 1999), 489.

3   J. M. Roberts, *Twentieth Century: The History of the World, 1901–Present* (New York: Penguin, 1999), 333.

4   Northwestern Alaska Chamber of Commerce, "Nome, Alaska," 1932, 9.

5   Allan, *Gold, Men and Dogs,* 237; Lomen, *Fifty Years in Alaska,* 145; and Charlotte Cameron, *A Cheechako in Alaska and Yukon* (London: T. Fisher Unwin, 1920), 247.

6   Carl J. Lomen diaries, February 1–22, 1910.

7   Cameron, *Cheechako in Alaska,* 247.

8   See "Nome Masonic Directory" in Nome Miscellanea Collection, University of Alaska Anchorage, Box 2; *Nome Industrial Worker,* April 3, 1917 and April 11, 1917.

9   See J. L. McLean, ed., "Report of the Alaska Pilgrimage of the Nile Temple," n.p., n.d.

10   Esther Birdsall Darling, *Up in Alaska* (Sacramento: Jo Anderson Press, 1912), 43.

11   Ibid., 18, 22, 27.

12   See chapter 2.

13   See the photographs in Choate and Harrison, "Chief Boatswain."

14   *Nome Nugget,* July 21, 1917; July 24, 1917.

15   *Daily Nome Industrial Worker,* December 10, 1915.

16   *Nome Nugget,* April 7, 1917.

17   *Daily Nome Industrial Worker,* April 4, 1917.

18　Ibid., December 27, 1915; April 3, 1917.

19　Haycox, *Alaska: An American Colony*, 210.

20　Spence, *Northern Gold Fleet*, 33, 34, 53, 54.

21　See *Daily Nome Industrial Worker*, April 3–17, 1917.

22　*Daily Nome Industrial Worker*, December 10, 1915.

23　*Nome Nugget*, July 25, 1917.

24　Frank Norris, "Alaskans and the Prohibition Experiment," in Alaska Historical Society, *Politics and Government in Alaska's Past* (Anchorage: Alaska Historical Society, 1995), 83–86.

25　*Nome Daily Nugget*, January 2, 1918.

26　*Daily Nome Industrial Worker*, April 13, 1917; *Nome Daily Nugget*, January 2, 1918.

27　*Nome Nugget*, July 22, 1916.

28　Ibid., December 24, 1917.

29　See, for example, Carl J. Lomen diaries, April 10–11, 1911; Rickard, *Through the Yukon and Alaska*, 321–26; and Shannon Garst, *"Scotty" Allan: King of the Dog-Team Drivers* (New York: J. Messner, 1946), 173.

30　Hunt, *North of 53*, 253–54.

31　*Aurora*, 1916, 47.

32　Nome Kennel Club, "All Alaska Sweepstakes, 1910," 2.

33　Ibid., 3–18, 20.

34　A. C. Edington, *Tundra: Romance and Adventure on Alaskan Trails* (New York: Century, 1930), viii–ix.

35　Hines, *Minstrel of the North*, 133.

36　*Aurora*, 1915, 34.

37　Ibid., 1914, 32

38　Ibid., 1915, 32.

39　*Aurora Borealis*, 1930 (Nome High School), 7.

40　*Aurora*, 1912.

41　Ibid., 1915, 11; 1916, 5.

42　Allan, *Gold, Men and Dogs*, 307. Allan was elected to the Nome School Board after the First World War. He does not tell us the substance of his run-ins with students' mothers but, having taught at the middle school and secondary levels, I assume that Nome's reform-minded parents were similar to the ones I have known. However pestiferous they may be, they are almost always motivated by a desire to have the best for their children. Of course, parents who do not care about education can also be difficult to deal with, but it is clear from Allan's text that those types were not his problem.

43　*Aurora*, 1905, 19.

44　Ibid., 1907, 11.

45　Ibid., 1915, 41.

46　Ibid., 1908, unnumbered insert.

47　Ibid., 1914, 54. In 1910, about 40 percent of American college students were women; by 1920 47 percent of college students were women. See Christopher J. Lucas, *American Higher Education: A History* (New York: St. Martin's Griffin, 1994), 206.

48　*Aurora*, 1907, 4.

49　Although parents were rebuked for not being interested enough "to turn aside from the money-getting and pleasure-seeking spirit of our city to stimulate and encourage these youthful and immortal minds in the acquisition of … knowledge." *Nome Pioneer Press*, September 15, 1908.

50　Barrett Willoughby, *The Trail Eater* (New York: G. P. Putnam's Sons, 1929), 6.

51   Reed, *Boyhood in the Nome Gold Camp*, 22.

52   Garst, *"Scotty" Allan*, 166.

53   *Aurora*, 1907, 4.

54   See Carl J. Lomen diaries, February 2, 1910; May 18, 1910; G. J. Lomen's unpublished speeches in Lomen Family Collection, Box 7, folder 120; and the high school's 1908 commencement speech reprinted in the *Nome Pioneer Press*, September 15, 1908.

55   The other two were Fairbanks and Juneau. Ketchikan, Skagway, Valdez, Cordova, Seward, and a nascent Anchorage had just one newspaper. See Gruening, *State of Alaska*, 217.

56   *Nome Industrial Worker*, December 13, 1915.

57   Ibid., December 8, 1915; December 15, 1915.

58   Ibid., December 21, 1918.

59   Ibid., December 28, 1918.

60   Joseph Sullivan, "Sourdough Radicalism: Labor and Socialism in Alaska, 1905–1920," *Alaska History* 7, no. 1 (Spring 1992): 3.

61   *Nome Nugget*, July 21, 1917.

62   Sullivan, "Sourdough Radicalism," 8–9, 12–13.

63.   See Sullivan, "Sourdough Radicalism."

64   *Nome Democrat*, February 22, 1914.

65   Haycox, *Alaska: An American Colony*, 223–30.

66   Hunt, *North of 53*, 223–24.

67   Spence, *Northern Gold Fleet*, 27.

68   Stearns, "The Morgan–Guggenheim Syndicate," 39–78.

69   State of Alaska, "Alaska Legislature Roster of Members, 1913–2000," December 2000.

70   *Nome Nugget*, July 5, 1917.

71   Carl J. Lomen diaries, April 1918 (no specific date given).

72   William R. Hunt, *Distant Justice: Policing the Alaska Frontier* (Norman: Univ. of Oklahoma Press, 1987), 224–25.

73   See the box of photographs titled "Non-Native Life," Carrie M. McLain Memorial Museum; for commentary preceding the induction, see Carl J. Lomen diaries, May 20, 1918.

74   For a longer discussion, see Jones, "Yankees in Parkas," 43–58.

75   See Ducker, "Out of Harm's Way," 43–64; and Mitchell, *Sold American*, 143–47.

76   Carl J. Lomen diaries, May 11, 1900.

77   Wirt, *Alaskan Adventures*, 55.

78   Reed, *Boyhood in the Nome Gold Camp*, 32.

79   Elizabeth Wood Albums, 1902–1914, Box 2.

80   See *Aurora*, 1910, 5–8, 29; Martin, *North to Nome*, 289; Madsen, *Arctic Trader*, 68; Ruthmary McDowell Papers, Box 1, folders 28, 32.

81   *Aurora*, 1910, 29.

82   Commencement exercise pamphlet, Nome High School, May 31, 1910, held at Anchorage Museum of History and Art.

83   *Aurora Borealis*, 1928, 28.

84   Helen Lomen, *Taktuk: An Arctic Boy* (Garden City: Doubleday, 1928).

85   Mitchell, *Sold American*, 143.

86   *Nome Nugget*, January 2, 1918.

87   See the quotation at the beginning of chapter 5.

88   This and following commentary on court cases refers to cases in Records of the Alaska Territorial Legislature, 1913–1953, file M1012, rolls 20 (cases 2171 and 2172), 34 (cases 2398,

2399, and 2405), 35 (cases 2423 and 2425), 47 (cases 2677, 2678, 2680, and 2682–2686), and 53 (cases 2770, 2773, and 2774).

89   Lawrence M. Friedman, *Law in America: A Short History* (New York: Modern Library, 2002), 165.

CHAPTER 5: STRUGGLE

1   *Aurora*, 1915, 37.
2   *Nome Nugget*, December 30, 1916.
3   Ibid., April 6, 1917.
4   *Tri-Weekly Nome Industrial Worker*, May 4, 1918.
5   The strikers wanted $5 a day plus board. A day's room rental at the Golden Gate in 1918 was about $2.50. I assume that standard rent was less than that and thus arrive at this figure. See Cameron, *Cheechako in Alaska*, 242; and *Tri-Weekly Nome Industrial Worker*, May 7, 1918.
6   *Tri-Weekly Nome Industrial Worker*, May 7, 1918.
7   Ibid., May 4, 1918.
8   Carl J. Lomen diaries, undated newspaper clipping, July 18, 1918.
9   *Tri-Weekly Nome Industrial Worker*, July 27, 1918.
10   Ibid., July 11, 1918.
11   Ibid., May 7, 1918.
12   Ibid., May 4, 1918.
13   Carl J. Lomen diaries, May 1917 (no specific date given).
14   Ibid., June 26, 1918.
15   *Nome Nugget*, April 9, 1917.
16   Ibid., October 25, 1918.
17   See the list of Alaska soldiers who died in the war in *Alaska Dispatch*, June 25, 1920. Seventy-six Alaskan soldiers died. Of these, just nine died overseas.
18   Cole, *Nome*, 135.
19   *Daily Nome Industrial Worker*, April 5, 1917.
20   *Nome Nugget*, April 9, 1917.
21   Spence, *Northern Gold Fleet*, 33, 34, 53, 54.
22   *Tri-Weekly Nome Industrial Worker*, May 9, 1918.
23   Ibid., July 13, 1918; August 29, 1918; July 27, 1918.
24   Borneman, *Alaska: Saga of a Bold Land*, 265.
25   Carl J. Lomen diaries, June 27, 1918.
26   Ibid., undated newspaper clipping, September 19, 1918.
27   Ibid., June 1918 (no specific date given).
28   Nichols, *Alaska*, 407.
29   Lyman L. Woodman, *Duty Station Northwest: The U.S. Army in Alaska and Western Canada, 1867–1987*, vol. 2 (Anchorage: Alaska Historical Society, 1997), 15.
30   See the next section.
31   Woodman, *Duty Station Northwest*, vol. 1, 316.
32   Returns from United States Military Post, 1800–1916, Fort Davis, Alaska, Jan. 1908–Dec. 1916, National Archives and Records Administration, file M617, roll 296.
33   Carl J. Lomen diaries, July 17, 1918. "Miss Jean Crowley marries Lieutenant Timothy Asbury Pedley of Fort Davis."
34   *Nome Tri-Weekly Nugget*, July 28, 1919.

35 See Washington B. Vanderlip and Homer B. Hulbert, *In Search of a Siberian Klondike* (New York: Century, 1903). Gold-mining operations received press outside Alaska as well. See, for example, Charles Janin, "Gold-Dredging in Russia," *Mining and Scientific Press*, January 6, 1912, 66; and K. I. Hlebnikoff, "Dredging on the Amur," *Mining and Scientific Press*, August 21, 1915, 283. In 1902, Herman Rosenthal referred to the "almost limitless mineral wealth of Siberia." See his "From New York to Paris by Rail," *Review of Reviews,* May 1906, 592.

36 *Daily Nome Industrial Worker*, April 30, 1917.

37 *Nome Tri-Weekly Nugget*, July 25, 1919. In the summer of 1917, before the Bolshevik Revolution, Charles Janin wrote that conditions in Russia could lead to "splendid opportunities for American capital." "The Russian Crisis," *Mining and Scientific Press*, August 4, 1917, 167.

38 T. A. Rickard, "The Russo-Asiatic Agreement," *Engineering and Mining Journal–Press*, November 11, 1922, 841.

39 On the latter point, see Linda Killen, *The Russian Bureau: A Case Study in Wilsonian Diplomacy* (Lexington: Univ. of Kentucky Press, 1983), 111.

40 Aleš Hrdlička, *Alaska Diary, 1926–1931* (Lancaster, PA: Jaques Cattell Press, 1943), 84.

41 Peter G. Boyle, *American-Soviet Relations* (New York: Routledge, 1993), 1–12, 17–19.

42 Woodman, *Duty Station Northwest*, vol. 2, 4.

43 For examples of the Lomens' Siberian views, see photographs #NC-1-43, NC-1-52, and NC-1-357 held at the Glenbow Museum in Calgary, Alberta.

44 *Nome Nugget*, July 26, 1916.

45 See the account of the American dentist robbed in Moscow in *Seward Gateway*, June 24, 1920.

46 William R. Hunt, *Alaska: A Bicentennial History* (New York: Norton, 1976), 71; and Mary J. Barry, "Captain Joseph Bernard, Arctic Trader," *Alaska Journal* 3, no. 4 (1973): 246–47.

47 Alphabetical Index of Alien Arrivals at Eagle, Hyder, Ketchikan, Nome, and Skagway, Alaska, June 1906–August 1946, file M2016, roll 1. The vast majority of immigrants to Alaska arrived in Ketchikan and Skagway. Others besides Russians entered at Nome—Canadians, Greeks, Germans, Swedes. But their numbers were very small.

48 Letter dated July 4, 1925, Wilson W. Brine Papers, Box 1.

49 *Nome Daily Gold Digger*, July 2, 1909; *Daily Nome Industrial Worker*, December 16, 1905.

50 Hunt, *Alaska: A Bicentennial History*, 73.

51 See Benson Lee Grayson, "Lost Opportunity: The Alaska Siberia Tunnel," *Asian Affairs* 64, no. 1 (1977): 67.

52 Hunt, *Alaska: A Bicentennial History*, 70. Called the Northeast Siberian Trading Company by Madsen, who also misspells the company's founder's name, John Rosene, as John Racine. See Madsen, *Arctic Trader*, 100.

53 Madsen, *Arctic Trader*, 56, 63, 144.

54 Carl J. Lomen diaries, September 17, 1910.

55 Louis H. Eisenlohr and Riley Wilson, *Memories: From Philadelphia to Charlestown, Maryland via Nome, Alaska* (Philadelphia: The Keystone Publishing Company, 1918), 59.

56 See Jan Welzl, *Thirty Years in the Golden North*, trans. Paul Selver (New York: Macmillan, 1932), 62 and 77; and clippings from *Pennsylvania Register*, January 31, 1924, in Harry and Ruth Dobson Papers, Box 1, file 11.

57 Madsen, *Arctic Trader*, 95–132.

58 *Nome Nugget*, July 12, 1916.

59 Ibid., July 21, 1916.

60 Victor Anderson, "Autobiography of Victor Anderson," unpublished manuscript, Carrie M. McLain Memorial Museum.

61 Carl J. Lomen diaries, September 12, 1919.

62 Woodman, *Duty Station Northwest*, vol. 1, 261, 310; Woodman, *Duty Station Northwest*, vol. 2, 15–16. On Siberia, see chapter 6.

63 Olaf Swenson, *Northwest of the World: Forty Years Trading and Hunting in Northern Siberia* (New York: Dodd, Mead and Co., 1944), 158–72.

64 Harry A. Frank, *The Lure of Alaska* (Garden City, NY: Blue Ribbon Books, 1943), 194.

65 Donald Chaput, "Gold for the Commissars: Charles Janin's Siberian Ventures," *Huntington Library Quarterly* 49, no. 4 (1986): 391.

66 Lomen, *Fifty Years in Alaska,* 163–67.

67 *Nome Nugget*, June 19, 1920.

68 *Alaska Dispatch*, June 25, 1920.

69 James Thomas Gay, "Some Observations of Eastern Siberia, 1922," *Slavonic and East European Review* 54, no. 135 (1976): 253.

70 *Nome Nugget*, June 26, 1920.

71 Swenson, *Northwest of the World*, 163–73; and Hunt, *Arctic Passage*, 207–10 and 267–87.

72 Lomen, *Fifty Years in Alaska*, 210–11.

73 Walter Irwin, unpublished journal, 1923, Lomen Family Collection, Miscellaneous, Box 36, folder 524.

74 Letter of June 29, 1923, in Wilson W. Brine Papers, Box 1, file "letters 1923."

75 Ira Harkey, *Noel Wien: Alaska Pioneer Bush Pilot* (Fairbanks: Univ. of Alaska Press, 1999), 233.

76 Vanderlip and Hulbert, *In Search of a Siberian Klondike*, 301.

77 C. W. Scarborough, "The Voyage that Failed," *Alaska Journal* 4, no. 1 (1974): 54.

78 Barry, "Captain Joseph Bernard," 247.

79 Ibid., 246.

80 Gay, "Some Observations," 256.

81 *Nome Nugget*, July 25, 1916; and Chaput, "Gold for the Commissars," 394.

82 Vanderlip and Hulbert, *In Search of a Siberian Klondike*, 3, 292; James M. Ashton, *Ice-Bound: A Trader's Adventures in the Siberian Arctic* (New York: G. P. Putnam's Sons, 1928), 18; Swenson, *Northwest of the World*, 13, 16–17, 127, 256; and Scarborough, "The Voyage that Failed," 50–53.

83 Northwestern Alaska Chamber of Commerce, "Nome, Alaska," 1932, 1.

84 *Nome Daily Nugget*, July 18, 1916.

85 House of Representatives, "Nome Harbor, Alaska," 22, 29.

86 Eisenlohr and Wilson, *Memories*, 61.

Chapter 6: Settling

1 *Daily Telegraph Bulletin*, August 9, 1923.

2 This is the title of chapter 7 in *Nome: "City of the Golden Beaches."*

3 Frank G. Carpenter, *Alaska, Our Northern Wonderland* (New York: Doubleday, Page, 1925), 185.

4 Ibid.

5 Hrdlička, *Alaska Diary*, 81.

6 See Kenneth A. Ungermann, *The Race to Nome: The Story of the Heroic Alaskan Dog Teams that Rushed Diphtheria Serum to Stricken Nome in 1925* (New York: Harper and Row, 1963); and Gay Salisbury and Laney Salisbury, *The Cruelest Miles: The Heroic Story of Dogs and Men in a Race against an Epidemic* (New York: Norton, 2003).

7 See William Hanable, "Nome's First Aerial Flight: The Alaska Flying Expedition of 1920," *Alaska History* 15, no. 2 (Fall 2000): 23.

8   Undated commencement address, Lomen Family Collection, Box 7, folder 120.

9   Harkey, *Noel Wien*, 191.

10   Hrdlička, *Alaska Diary*, 84.

11   See "Directory, Nome Federal Business Association, 1926–1927" in Lomen Family Collection, Box 7, folder 114.

12   Northwestern Alaska Chamber of Commerce, "Nome, Alaska," 1932, 5.

13   Hrdlička, *Alaska Diary*, 81.

14   Spence, *Northern Gold Fleet*, 70.

15   House of Representatives, "Nome Harbor, Alaska," 22.

16   Ibid., 16, 23.

17   Cole, *Nome*, 140.

18   *Nome Nugget*, April 11, 1917.

19   *Nome Nugget*, July 25, 1917.

20   A. W. Greeley, *Handbook of Alaska: Its Resources, Products, and Attractions in 1924* (Port Washington, NY: Kennikat, 1925), 43.

21   Ibid., 42; and Carpenter, *Alaska: Our Northern Wonderland*, 139.

22   Hunt, *North of 53*, 255.

23   Woodman, *Duty Station Northwest*, vol. 2, 49.

24   These figures are taken from Alaska Road Commission, "Annual Report," (1936), 2, 17, 19, 23, 24, 35, 49.

25   Jonathan M. Nielson, *Armed Forces on a Northern Frontier: The Military in Alaska's History, 1867–1987* (New York: Greenwood, 1988), 139.

26   See Carrigher, *Moonlight at Midday*, 261. I make the latter claim based on my conversations with residents of Nome in June of 2004.

27   Claim based on informal conversations I had with residents of Nome in the summer of 2004.

28   NARA. Records of the Alaska Territorial Legislature, 1913–1953, file M1012, roll 1.

29   *Nome Nugget*, July 24, 1916.

30   *Nome Tri-Weekly Nugget,* July 25, 1919.

31   Lyman L. Woodman, "Nome Harbor," *Alaska Journal* 6, no. 4 (Autumn 1976): 200.

32   Ibid., 207.

33   House of Representatives, "Mouth of Snake River and Nome Harbor, Alaska," 64th Congress, 2nd session, document no. 1932.

34   File "Nome Jetty" held at Carrie M. McLain Memorial Museum.

35   Woodman, "Nome Harbor," 208.

36   Carl J. Lomen diaries, September 26, 1919.

37   Ibid., June 2, 1920.

38   Ibid., September 8, 1920.

39   Woodman, *Duty Station Northwest*, vol. 2, 4.

40   See Shiels, *Seward's Icebox*, 166–83.

41   Eisenlohr and Wilson, *Memories*, 63; and Northwestern Alaska Chamber of Commerce, "Nome, Alaska," 1932, 39.

42   *Nome Nugget*, July 25, 1919.

43   Quoted in Hunt, *Arctic Passage*, 216. Vilhjalmur Stefansson was somewhat less effusive when he declared that the herding of reindeer and musk oxen on Baffin Island would make "northern Canada the great wool-, meat-, and milk-producing area of the western hemisphere." *Discovery*, 265.

44   Lomen Family Collection, Box 7, folder 120.

45   Stefansson, *Northward Course of Empire*, 60.

46   Stefansson, *Discovery*, 262; and Stefansson, *Adventure of Wrangel Island*, 299–303.

47   Greeley, *Handbook of Alaska*, 161.

48   Ibid., 165. The journalist Trumbull White used similar language, writing that the Eskimos, thanks partly to the reindeer industry, had "recently emerged from darkness, and of a mental maturity not beyond the lower grammar school grades, even though they are astute, intelligent, gentle trusting and trustworthy." See White's "Coming Storm over Alaska," *New Outlook* 169, no. 7 (August 1933): 20.

49   White, "Coming Storm over Alaska," 20.

50   Lomen, *Fifty Years in Alaska*, 78.

51   Stefansson, *Northward Course of Empire*, 58.

52   Carl Lomen says as much in *Fifty Years in Alaska*, 88.

53   See the photograph in Cole, *Nome*, 152.

54   Thames Williamson, *On the Reindeer Trail* (New York: Houghton Mifflin, 1932), dedication page; and Max Miller, *The Great Trek: The Story of the Five-Year Drive of a Reindeer Herd through the Icy Wastes of Alaska and Northwestern Canada* (New York: Doubleday, Doran, 1935), 14.

55   See, for example, House of Representatives, "Nome Harbor, Alaska," 4, 17, and 24.

56   Stefansson, *Northward Course of Empire*, 59.

57   I examined Department of the Interior, *Survey of the Alaska Reindeer Service, 1931–1933* (Washington, DC, 1934); and Lawrence Palmer, *Raising Reindeer in Alaska* (Washington, DC, 1934).

58   Mitchell, *Sold American*, 143–48; and Ducker, "Out of Harm's Way."

59   Rickard, *Through the Yukon and Alaska*, 318; and Reed, *Boyhood in the Nome Gold Camp*, 24.

60   See letter dated November 20, 1930, Carl J. Lomen File, Box 11, Lomen Family Collection.

61   Lomen, *Fifty Years in Alaska*, 89.

62   Such is my theory based on a hunch well-informed by immersion in the sources.

63   See Lomen, *Fifty Years in Alaska*, 213; and C. L. Andrews, *The Eskimo and His Reindeer in Alaska* (Caldwell, ID: Caxton, 1939), 197.

64   Carl J. Lomen diaries, September 28 and October 21, 1920.

65   House of Representatives, "Nome Harbor, Alaska," 24.

66   Lomen, *Fifty Years in Alaska*, 78, 173.

67   Ibid., 282.

68   Vilhjalmur Stefansson, *The Friendly Arctic: The Story of Five Years in Polar Regions* (New York: Greenwood, 1969), 697–98.

69   Cole, *Nome*, 105.

70   See the box of photographs titled "Disasters" in the Carrie M. McLain Memorial Museum.

71   "Nomania," 1938. Published by locals for locals. Copy held in Carrie M. McLain Memorial Museum.

72   Northwestern Alaska Chamber of Commerce, "Nome, Alaska," 1932, 4.

73   Ibid., passim.

74   Unless otherwise indicated, all information in the following paragraphs is drawn from the *Nome Nugget* of September 15, 1934.

75   *Nome Nugget*, December 17, 1941.

76   *Anchorage Daily News*, September 18, 1934.

77   Department of the Interior, "Territorial, Alaska, Nome Disaster," RG126, Box 383, classified files, 1907–1951, file 9-1-58.

78   "The Nome, Alaska, Fire of September 17, 1934," Red Cross official report.

79   *Anchorage Daily News*, September 18, 1934; and see the photograph in Cole, *Nome*, 158.

80   Bowen McCoy, Red Cross relief effort director in Nome, to A. L. Schafer, manager of the
      Red Cross's Pacific Branch office, September 29, 1934.

81   Unsigned, undated, untitled document listing federal buildings destroyed. Department of
      the Interior, "Territorial, Alaska, Nome Disaster," RG126, Box 383, classified files, 1907–
      1951, file 9-1-58.

82   *Nome Daily Nugget*, November 10, 1934; and R. Bruce Parham, "Bankruptcy Case Files of
      the U.S. District Court of the District Court for the District and Territory of Alaska, Second
      Division, 1901–1953," National Archives and Records Administration, 1998, 5.

83   *Anchorage Daily News*, September 18, 1934.

84   Cole, *Nome*, 159.

85   *New York Times*, September 18, 1934.

86   Telegram is reproduced in Cole, *Nome*, 157.

87   See the advertisement in *Nome Daily Nugget*, November 12, 1934.

88   *Anchorage Daily News*, September 19, 1934.

89   *Seward Gateway*, September 20, 1934.

90   *Anchorage Daily News*, September 19, 1934.

91   Gruening, *State of Alaska*, 300.

92   Troy to Ickes, September 18, 1934, Department of the Interior, "Territorial, Alaska, Nome
      Disaster," RG126, Box 383, classified files, 1907–1951, file 9-1-58.

93   See, for example, Harry L. Harper to Ickes, September 26, 1934; R. B. Bain to Ickes, October 1,
      1934; and Seattle Sour Dough Club to Ickes, September 28, 1934, Department of the Interior,
      "Territorial, Alaska, Nome Disaster." RG126, box 383, classified files, 1907–1951, file 9-1-58.

94   "The Nome, Alaska, Fire of September 17, 1934," Department of the Interior, "Territorial,
      Alaska, Nome Disaster." RG126, box 383, classified files, 1907–1951, file 9-1-58.

95   McCoy to A. L. Schafer, September 25, 1934, Department of the Interior, "Territorial,
      Alaska, Nome Disaster." RG126, box 383, classified files, 1907–1951, file 9-1-58.

96   J. A. Hellenthal, *The Alaskan Melodrama* (New York: Liveright Publishing Corporation,
      1936), 3.

97   Ralph Lomen to Carl Lomen, September 19, 1934, Department of the Interior, "Territorial,
      Alaska, Nome Disaster," RG126, Box 383, classified files, 1907–1951, file 9-1-58.

98   John Troy to Harold Ickes, September 18, 1934, Department of the Interior, "Territorial,
      Alaska, Nome Disaster," RG126, Box 383, classified files, 1907–1951, file 9-1-58.

99   See the Interior Department's reply, April 22, 1935, Department of the Interior, "Territorial,
      Alaska, Nome Disaster," RG126, Box 383, classified files, 1907–1951, file 9-1-58.

100   See, for example, Harrison to Department of the Interior, March 4, 1935, Department of
      the Interior, "Territorial, Alaska, Nome Disaster," RG126, Box 383, classified files, 1907–
      1951, file 9-1-58.

101   Ziehl to Department of the Interior, January 14, 1935, Department of the Interior, "Territorial,
      Alaska, Nome Disaster," RG126, Box 383, classified files, 1907–1951, file 9-1-58.

102   Schorn to Department of the Interior, January 10, 1935, Department of the Interior,
      "Territorial, Alaska, Nome Disaster," RG126, Box 383, classified files, 1907–1951, file 9-1-58.

103   Memo to Ernest Gruening, September 22, 1934, Department of the Interior, "Territorial,
      Alaska, Nome Disaster," RG126, Box 383, classified files, 1907–1951, file 9-1-58.

104   *Nome Daily Nugget*, November 8, 1934.

105   Ibid., December 24, 1934.

106   For views of the Golden Gate Hotel and the interior of a Nome bank, circa 1900, see Claus-
      M. Naske and Ludwig J. Rowinski, *Alaska: A Pictorial History* (Virginia Beach: Donning,
      1983), 111, 113.

CONCLUSION

1 Kitchener, *Flag over the North*, 243; Woodman, *Duty Station Northwest*, vol. 1, 322.

2 Louis Jacobin, "There's No Place Like Nome" *Alaska Life*, May 1945, 23.

3 Kitchener, *Flag over the North*, 232–34, 237, 252.

4 Herb and Miriam Hilscher, *Alaska, U.S.A.* (Boston: Little, Brown, 1959), 40.

5 See George Sundborg, *Opportunity in Alaska* (New York: Macmillan, 1945), 168, 194, 206, 208, 209.

6 Will H. Chase, *Pioneers of Alaska: The Trail-Blazers of Bygone Days* (Kansas City, MO: Burton, 1951), 85–113.

7 *Anchorage Daily News*, September 18, 1934.

8 Allan, *Gold, Men and Dogs*, 55, 145, 152.

9 Julia Scully, *Outside Passage: A Memoir of an Alaskan Childhood* (New York: Random House, 1998), 50, 57.

10 See Orlando Miller, *The Frontier in Alaska and the Matanuska Colony* (New Haven: Yale Univ. Press, 1975), 162–73. The *Daily News-Miner* is quoted on page 168.

11 Borneman, *Alaska: Saga of a Bold Land*, 341.

12 Miller, *Frontier in Alaska*, 180.

13 See the chapter with that title in Joseph Driscoll, *War Discovers Alaska* (Philadelphia: Lippincott, 1944). On page 76 Driscoll writes: "Now that we are striking back with increasing intensity at the enemy in the North Pacific as well as in the South Seas, the people in the United States may begin to appreciate that Alaska was worth saving and that the Japanese thrust into the Aleutians was not a face-saving gesture but a real threat to the whole continent."

14 Ralph Lomen, "Talk on Alaska," in Lomen Family Collection, Box 7, folder 121.

15 Hines, *Minstrel of the Yukon*, 231. Nome is where the rapist of Hines's wife first became acquainted with the couple, so the claim seems a little disingenuous. Hines later murdered the rapist in the Outside, though he was not convicted by a jury.

16 Stephen Haycox, *Warm Past: Travels in Alaska History* (Anchorage: Press North, 1988), 32–34.

17 Haycox, *Alaska: An American Colony*.

18 Claus-M. Naske, *Alaska: A History of the 49th State* (Norman: Univ. of Oklahoma Press, 1987), 107–8, 174.

19 Borneman, *Alaska: Saga of a Bold Land*, 273–77, 293, 295, 298, 353.

20 Jacobin, "There's No Place Like Nome," 10.

21 See, for example, Bryan Cooper, *Alaska: The Last Frontier* (New York: William Morrow, 1973), 62; and Naske and Rowinski, *Alaska: A Pictorial History*, 111–15.

22 Carrigher, *Moonlight at Midday*, 3, 6, 205, 250, 256, 267, 275, 282–83, 304.

23 Cooper, *Alaska: The Last Frontier*, 190.

24 Wharton, *Alaska Gold Rush*, 208–10.

25 Scully, *Outside Passage*, 28, 122, 134, 159, 199–200.

26 Terrence Cole exaggerates racial separatism in mid-century Nome, although his essay "Jim Crow in Alaska: The Passage of the Alaska Equal Rights Act of 1945" in *An Alaska Anthology: Interpreting the Past*, ed. Stephen W. Haycox and Mary Childers Mangusso (Seattle: Univ. of Washington Press, 1996) is useful. See especially pages 316 and 327.

27 General photograph file, Anchorage Museum of Art and History, photo number B00.8.10.

28 See Jones, "Yankees in Parkas."

29 Kitchener, *Flag over the North*, 233; and Gruening, *State of Alaska*, 376.

BIBLIOGRAPHY

ABBREVIATIONS

AMHA: Anchorage Museum of History and Art

AML: Anchorage Municipal Library

CM: Carrie M. McLain Memorial Museum, Nome

NARA-PAR: National Archives and Records Administration, Pacific Alaska Region (Anchorage)

NARA-CP: National Archives and Records Administration, College Park, Maryland

UAA: University of Alaska Anchorage

UAF: University of Alaska Fairbanks

ARCHIVAL MATERIALS

Arthur Bell and other photographic collections (CM)

Aurora (later *Aurora Borealis*), Nome High School, 1907–1928 (CM, AMHA, UAF)

Elizabeth Wood Albums (UAF)

E. S. Harrison, "Alaska Basketball Team Touring the United States" (CM)

General photograph file (AMHA)

Lomen Family Collection (UAF)

Nome High School commencement exercise pamphlet, 1910 (AMHA)

Nome Kennel Club, "All Alaska Sweepstakes 1910" (AMHA)

O. D. Goetze Collection (AMHA)

Ruth and Harry Dobson Papers (UAA)

Ruthmary McDowell Papers (UAF)

Wilson W. Brine Papers (UAA)

GOVERNMENT RECORDS

Admiralty Case Files of the U.S. District Court for the District and Territory of Alaska, Second Division. Record Group 21; publication number M1967. (NARA-PAR)

Alaska File of the Revenue Cutter Service. Record Group 26; publication number M641. (NARA-PAR)

Alaska File of the Special Agents Division of the Department of the Treasury, publication number M802. (NARA-PAR)

Alaska Road Commission, Annual Report, 1936 (AML)

Alphabetical Index of Alien Arrivals at Eagle, Hyder, Ketchikan, Nome and Skagway, Alaska, June 1906-August 1946. Publication number M2106. (NARA-PAR)

Bankruptcy Case Files of the U.S. District Court for the District and Territory of Alaska, Second Division. Record Group 21; publication number M1966. (NARA-PAR)

Civil Case Files of the U.S. District Court for the District and Territory of Alaska, Second Division. Record Group 21; publication number I20. (NARA-PAR)

Correspondence of the Secretary of Alaska. Publication number T1201. (NARA-PAR)

General Correspondence of the Governor of Alaska. Publication number M939. (NARA-PAR)

House of Representatives, "Mouth of Snake River and Nome Harbor, Alaska." 64th Congress, 2nd session.

———, "Nome Harbor, Alaska." 71st Congress, 2nd session.

Interior Department, "Survey of the Alaska Reindeer Service, 1931–1933." Washington, DC, 1934.

———, "Territorial, Alaska, Nome Disaster," Record group 126. (NARA-CP)

Interior Department Territorial Papers. Record group, 48; publication number M430. (NARA-PAR)

Records of the Alaska Territorial Legislature. Record group 348, publication number M1012 (NARA-PAR)

State of Alaska, "Alaska Legislature Roster of Members, 1913–2000," 2000. (AML)

NEWSPAPERS

Alaska Dispatch (Seattle)

Alaska Free Press (Juneau)

Alaska Journal (Juneau)

Alaska Miner (Juneau)

Anchorage Daily News

Arctic Midnight Sun (Nome)

Council City News

Daily Alaskan (Skagway)

Daily Telegraph Bulletin (Nome)

Dyea Trail

Fairbanks Daily News-Miner

Fort Wrangel News

Nome Chronicle (Nov. 14, 1900–June 18, 1901)

Nome Daily Chronicle (Aug. 11–Sept. 29, 1900)

Nome Weekly Chronicle (Oct. 6–Nov. 10, 1900)

Nome Democrat

Nome Gold Digger

Daily Nome Industrial Worker. Variant titles: *Nome Industrial Worker; Tri-Weekly Nome Industrial Worker*

Nome News

Nome Nugget. Variant titles: *Nome Daily Nugget; Nome Semi-Weekly Nugget; Nome Tri-Weekly Nugget*

Nome Pioneer Press. Variant title: *Nome Morning Pioneer Press*

Seward Gateway

Skaguay News

Teller News

UNPUBLISHED MANUSCRIPTS

Anderson, Victor. "Autobiography of Victor Anderson." (CM)

Choate, Glenda, and Thomas Harrison. "Chief Boatswain Thomas Austin Ross and the U.S. Life Saving Station, Nome, Alaska, 1905–1935." (AML)

Ducker, James. "Gold-Rushers to the North: The People of Nome in 1900." (AML)

McLean, J. L. "Report of the Alaska Pilgrimage of the Nile Temple." (UAA)

Mohr, Joan Antonson. "Alaska and the Sea: A Survey of Alaska's Maritime History." Anchorage: Office of History and Archaeology, 1979.

"Nomania," 1938. (CM)

"Nome Jetty." (CM)

Nome Kennel Club, "All Alaska Sweepstakes, 1910." (AMHA)

Norris, Frank. "Alaskans and the Prohibition Experiment." Alaska Historical Society, *Politics and Government in Alaska's Past*, 1995. (AML)

Northwestern Alaska Chamber of Commerce, "Nome, Alaska," 1932. (AMHA)

Rollins, Alden M., ed. "Census Alaska: Numbers of Inhabitants, 1792–1970." University of Alaska Anchorage Library, 1978.

Theses and Dissertations

Burch, Franklin Ward. "Alaska's Railroad Frontier: Railroads and Federal Development Policy, 1898–1915." PhD diss., Catholic University of America, 1965.

Cole, Terrence. "A History of the Nome Gold Rush: The Poor Man's Paradise." PhD diss., University of Washington, 1983.

Poling, John Marion. "A History of the Nome, Alaska, Public Schools, 1899–1958." Master's thesis, University of Alaska, 1970.

Shortridge, James R. "American Perceptions of the Agricultural Potential of Alaska, 1867–1958." PhD diss., University of Kansas, 1972.

Stearns, Robert Alden. "The Morgan–Guggenheim Syndicate and the Development of Alaska, 1906–1915." PhD diss., University of California, Santa Barbara, 1967.

Williams, Gerald O. "Michael J. Healy and the Alaska Maritime Frontier, 1880–1902." PhD diss., University of Oregon, 1987.

Articles and Book Chapters

Adams, George Edward. "Cape Nome Beach and Tundra Placer Mines." *Harper's Weekly*, August 4, 1900, 724–26.

———. "Cape Nome's Wonderful Placer Mines." *Harper's Weekly*, June 9, 1900, 529–31.

Alberts, Laurie. "Petticoats and Pickaxes: Who Were the Women that Joined the Klondike Gold Rush?" *Alaska Journal* 7, no. 3 (Summer 1977): 146–59.

Bailey, Thomas A. "The Discovery of Gold at Nome, Alaska." In *Alaska and Its History*, edited by Morgan B. Sherwood (Seattle: Univ. of Washington Press, 1967).

Barry, Mary J. "Captain Joseph Bernard, Arctic Trader." *Alaska Journal* 3, no. 4 (1973): 246–51.

Bolotin, Norm. "Nome's 1907 Version of the Globetrotters." *Alaska Journal* 9, no. 4 (Autumn 1979): 64–67.

Castle, N. H. "A Short History of Council and Cheenik." *Alaska Pioneer* 1, no. 1 (June 1912): 8–14.

Chaput, Donald. "Gold for the Commissars: Charles Janin's Siberian Ventures." *Huntington Library Quarterly* 49, no. 4 (1986): 385–400.

Cole, Terrence. "Baseball Above and Below Zero: The National Pastime in Alaska." *Alaska Journal* 13, no. 3 (Summer 1983): 129–35.

———. "The Bridge to Tomorrow: Visions of the Bering Strait Bridge." *Alaska History* 5, no. 2 (Fall 1990): 1–15.

———. "Jim Crow in Alaska: The Passage of the Alaska Equal Rights Act of 1945." In *An Alaska Anthology: Interpreting the Past*, edited by Stephen W. Haycox and Mary Childers Mangusso (Seattle: Univ. of Washington Press, 1996).

———. "Promoting the Pacific Rim: The Alaska–Yukon–Pacific Exposition of 1909." *Alaska History* 6, no. 1 (Spring 1991): 18–34.

Ducker, James. "A Census Study of the Yukon and Alaskan Gold Rushes, 1896–1900." In *An Alaska Anthology: Interpreting the Past*, edited by Stephen W. Haycox and Mary Childers Mangusso (Seattle: Univ. of Washington Press, 1996).

———. "Gold Rushers North: A Census Study of the Yukon and Alaskan Gold Rushes, 1896–1900." *Pacific Northwest Quarterly* 85, no. 3 (July 1994): 82–91.

———. "Out of Harm's Way: Relocating Northwest Alaska Eskimos, 1907–1917." *American Indian Culture and Research Journal* 20, no. 1 (1996): 43–64.

Foster, James C. "AFL, IWW and Nome: 1905–1908." *Alaska Journal* 5, no. 2 (Spring 1975): 66–73.

Freidel, Frank. "Dissent in the Spanish-American War and the Philippine Insurrection." In *Dissent in Three American Wars*, edited by Samuel Eliot Morison, Frederick Merk, and Frank Freidel (Cambridge, MA: Harvard Univ. Press, 1970).

Gay, James Thomas. "Some Observations of Eastern Siberia, 1922," *Slavonic and East European Review* 54, no. 135 (1976): 248–61.

Gibbs, George S. "Transportation Methods in Alaska," *National Geographic Magazine* 17, no. 2 (February 1906).

Grayson, Benson Lee. "Lost Opportunity: The Alaska Siberia Tunnel," *Asian Affairs* 64, no.1 (1977): 63–69.

Hanable, William. "Nome's First Aerial Flight: The Alaska Flying Expedition of 1920," *Alaska History* 15, no. 2 (Fall 2000): 20–28.

Hansome, Marius. "The Eskimo and the Fourth 'R'," *Current History* 16, no. 103 (April 22, 1922): 103–7.

Hlebnikoff, K. I. "Dredging on the Amur," *Mining and Scientific Press*, August 21, 1915, 283.

Jacobin, Louis. "There's No Place Like Nome," *Alaska Life*, May 1945: 3–23.

Janin, Charles. "Gold-Dredging in Russia," *Mining and Scientific Press*, January 6, 1912, 66–67.
———. "The Russian Crisis," *Mining and Scientific Press*, August 4, 1917, 163–67.

Jones, Preston. "At the Edge of Empire: Forging Americanness in Nome, 1899–1905," *Alaska History* 19, nos. 1–2 (Spring/Fall 2004): 25–43.
———. "Yankees in Parkas: Native Influence at Nome, 1900–1920," *Alaska History* 20, no. 2 (Fall 2005): 43–58.

Kunkel, Jeff. "The Two Eskimo Boys Meet the Three Lucky Swedes," Nome: Sitnasuak Native Corporation and Anchorage: Glacier House Publications, 2002.

Leta M. Hamilton, "Our Nome Honeymoon in 1931," *Alaska Journal* 16 (1986): 11–12.

Marks, Paula Mitchell. "The Age of Gold." In *Precious Dust: The American Gold Rush Era, 1848–1900* (New York: William Morrow and Co., 1994).

Merrick, Frank L. "The Alaska–Yukon–Pacific Exposition," *Alaska–Yukon Magazine* 2, no. 3 (September 1906): 2.

Murtagh, William J. "Some Homes of Nome," *Alaska Journal* 4, no. 1 (Winter 1974): 17–20.

Noble, Dennis L. "The Arctic Adventures of the *Thetis*," *Arctic* 30, no. 1 (1977): 3–12.

Osborne, Alice. "The Council City and Solomon River Railroad," *Alaska Journal* 5, no. 1 (Winter 1975): 49–54.

"Pour s'aboucher au G. T. Pacifique," *Le Journal du Madawaska* (Van Buren, ME), August 19, 1903, 2.

Rickard, T. A. "The Russo-Asiatic Agreement," *Engineering and Mining Journal-Press*, November 11, 1922, 840–41.

Rosenthal, Herman. "From New York to Paris by Rail," *Review of Reviews*, May 1906: 592–93.

Scarborough, C. W. "The Voyage that Failed," *Alaska Journal* 4, no. 1 (1974): 49–59.

Sherwood, Morgan. "A North Pacific Bubble, 1902–1907," *Alaska History* 12, no. 1 (Spring 1997): 18–31.

Spence, Clark C. "The Ernst–Alaska Dredging Company: Small Dredge Technology on the Nome Beaches, 1910–1920," *Alaska History* 2, no. 1 (Winter 1986/87): 1–15.

Sullivan, Joseph. "Sourdough Radicalism: Labor and Socialism in Alaska, 1905–1920," *Alaska History* 7, no. 1 (Spring 1992): 1–15.

"Une voie ferree de la Baie d'Hudson a [*sic*] Buenos-Ayres," *Le Journal du Madawaska* (Van Buren, ME), September 2, 1903, 2.

White, Trumbull. "Coming Storm over Alaska," *New Outlook* 169, no. 17 (August 1933): 16–21.

Wilson, William H. "The Serum Dash to Nome, 1925," *Alaska Journal* 16 (1986): 251–59.

Woodman, Lyman L. "Nome Harbor," *Alaska Journal* 6, no. 4 (Autumn 1976): 199–209.

BOOKS

Allan, A. A. "Scotty." *Gold, Men and Dogs*. New York: G. P. Putnam, 1931.

Andrews, C. L. *The Eskimo and His Reindeer in Alaska*. Caldwell, ID: Caxton, 1939.

Ashton, James M. *Ice-Bound: A Trader's Adventures in the Siberian Arctic*. New York: G. P. Putnam, 1928.

Atwood, Evangeline. *Frontier Politics: Alaska's James Wickersham*. Portland, OR: Binford and Mort, 1979.

Barbeau, Marius. *Alaska Beckons*. Caldwell, ID: Caxton, 1947.

Benfy, Christopher. *The Great Wave: Gilded Age Misfits, Japanese Eccentrics, and the Opening of Old Japan*. New York: Random House, 2003.

Berger, Carl. *The Sense of Power: Studies in the Ideas of Canadian Imperialism, 1867–1914*. Toronto: Univ. of Toronto Press, 1970.

Berton, Pierre. *The Klondike Fever: The Life and Death of the Last Gold Rush*. 1958. Reprint, New York: Carroll and Graf, 2000.

Bone, Scott C. *Chechahco and Sourdough: A Story of Alaska*. Atascadero, CA: Western, 1926.

Borneman, Walter R. *Alaska: Saga of a Bold Land*. New York: HarperCollins, 2003.

Boyle, Peter G. *American–Soviet Relations*. New York: Routledge, 1993.

Brooks, Alfred H. et al. *Mineral Resources in Alaska, 1916*. Washington, DC: Government Printing Office, 1918.

Brown, Robert Craig, and Ramsay Cook. *Canada, 1896–1921: A Nation Transformed*. Toronto: McClelland and Stewart, 1991.

Cameron, Charlotte. *A Cheechako in Alaska and Yukon*. London: T. Fisher Unwin, 1920.

Carpenter, Frank G. *Alaska: Our Northern Wonderland*. New York: Doubleday, Page, 1925.

Carrigher, Sally. *Moonlight at Midday*. New York: Knopf, 1959.

Chase, Will H. *Pioneers of Alaska: The Trail-Blazers of Bygone Days*. Kansas City, MO: Burton, 1951.

Cherry, Conrad, ed. *God's New Israel: Religious Interpretations of American Destiny*. Chapel Hill: Univ. of North Carolina Press, 1998.

Clark, M. *Roadhouse Tales; or, Nome in 1900*. Girard, KS: Appeal Publishing, 1902.

Clifford, Howard. *Rails North: The Railroads of Alaska and the Yukon*. Seattle: Superior Publishing, 1981.

Cobb, Norma, and Charles Sasser. *Arctic Homestead: The True Story of One Family's Survival and Courage in the Alaskan Wilds*. New York: St. Martin's, 2003.

Coffin, Charles Carleton. *The Seat of Empire*. Boston: Fields, Osgood, 1870.

Cohen, Stan. *Gold Rush Gateway: Skagway and Dyea, Alaska*. Missoula: Pictorial Histories, 1986.

Cole, Terrence. *Nome: "City of Golden Beaches."* Anchorage: Alaska Geographic Society, 1984.

———. *Wheels on Ice: Bicycling in Alaska, 1898–1908*. Anchorage: Alaska Northwest, 1985.

Colley, Linda. *Captives*. New York: Pantheon Books, 2002.

Cook, Ramsay, ed. *French Canadian Nationalism: An Anthology*. Toronto: Macmillan of Canada, 1969.

Cooper, Bryan. *Alaska: The Last Frontier*. New York: Morrow, 1973.

Cuba, Lee J. *Identity and Community on the Alaskan Frontier*. Philadelphia: Temple Univ. Press, 1987.

Dalton, Kathleen, *Theodore Roosevelt: A Strenuous Life*. New York: Knopf, 2002.

Darling, Esther Birdsall. *Baldy of Nome*. Philadelphia: Penn Publishing Co., 1917.
———. *Up in Alaska*. Sacramento: Jo Anderson Press, 1912.

Davis, Mary Lee. *Uncle Sam's Attic: The Intimate Story of Alaska*. Boston: W. A. Wilde, 1930.

De Windt, Harry. *Through the Gold Fields of Alaska and Bering Straits*. London: Chatto and Windus, 1899.

DeWitt, Johanna. *The Littlest Reindeer*. Chicago: Children's Press, 1946.

Dickey, R. M. *Gold Fever: The Narrative of the Great Klondike Gold Rush, 1897–1899*. Auke Bay, AK: Klondike Research, 1997.

Driscoll, Joseph. *War Discovers Alaska*. Philadelphia: Lippincott, 1944.

Dunham, Sam C. *The Alaskan Goldfields*. 1958. Reprint, Anchorage: Alaska Northwest, 1983.
———. *The Goldsmith of Nome*. Washington, DC: Neale, 1901.

Edington, A. C. *Tundra: Romance and Adventure on Alaskan Trails*. New York: Century, 1930.

Eisenlohr, Louis, and Riley Wilson. *Memories: From Philadelphia to Charlestown, Maryland via Nome, Alaska*. Philadelphia: The Keystone Publishing Company, 1918.

Emanuel, Richard P. *The Golden Gamble*. Anchorage: Alaska Geographic, 1997.

Fortuine, Robert. *Chills and Fever: Health and Disease in the Early History of Alaska*. Fairbanks: Univ. of Alaska Press, 1989.

Frank, Harry A. *The Lure of Alaska*. Garden City, NY: Blue Ribbon Books, 1943.

Fraser, J. D. *The Gold Fever; or, Two Years in Alaska*. Honolulu: 1923.

French, L. H. *Nome Nuggets*. 1905. Reprint, Anchorage: Alaska Northwest, 1983.

Friedman, Lawrence M. *Law in America: A Short History*. New York: Modern Library, 2002.

Gallagher, Dan. *Florida's Great Ocean Railway: Building the Key West Extension*. Sarasota, FL: Pineapple Press, 2003.

Garst, Shannon. *"Scotty" Allan: King of the Dog-Team Drivers*. New York: J. Messner, 1946.

George, Marian M. *Little Journeys to Alaska and Canada*. Chicago: A. Flanagan, 1901.

Gibson, Arrell Morgan. *Yankees in Paradise: The Pacific Basin Frontier*. Albuquerque: Univ. of New Mexico Press, 1993.

Gilpin, William. *Cosmopolitan Railway Compacting and Fusing Together All the World's Continents*. San Francisco: History Co., 1890.

Goulet, Emil Oliver. *Rugged Years on the Alaska Frontier*. Philadelphia: Dorrance, 1949.

Greely, A. W. *Handbook of Alaska: Its Resources, Products, and Attractions in 1924*. Port Washington, NY: Kennikat, 1925.

Gruening, Ernest. *The State of Alaska: A Definitive History of America's Northernmost Frontier*. New York: Random House, 1968.

Hader, Berta, and Elmer Hader. *Reindeer Trail: A Long Journey from Lapland to Alaska*. New York: Macmillan, 1959.

Haigh, Jane G. *Alaska Pioneer Interiors*. Fairbanks: Tanana-Yukon Historical Society, 1986.

Harkey, Ira. *Noel Wien: Alaska Pioneer Bush Pilot*. 1974. Reprint, Fairbanks: Univ. of Alaska Press, 1999.

Harrison, E. S. *Nome and Seward Peninsula*. Seattle: Metropolitan Press, 1905.

Haycox, Stephen. *Alaska: An American Colony*. Seattle: Univ. of Washington Press, 2002.
———. *Frigid Embrace: Politics, Economics and Environmentalism in Alaska*. Corvallis: Oregon State Univ. Press, 2002.
———. *Warm Past: Travels in Alaska History*. Anchorage: Press North, 1988.

Heffer, Jean. *The United States and the Pacific: History of a Frontier*. Trans. W. Donald Wilson. South Bend: Univ. of Notre Dame Press, 2002.

Hegg, L. A. *Souvenir of Alaska*. Seattle: 1900.

Hellenthal, J. A. *The Alaskan Melodrama*. New York: Liveright, 1936.

Henderson, Alice Palmer. *The Rainbow's End: Alaska*. New York: Herbert S. Stone, 1898.

Herron, Edward. *Alaska: Land of Tomorrow*. New York: McGraw-Hill, 1947.

Higginson, Ella. *Alaska: The Great Country*. New York: Macmillan, 1908.

Hill, Robert. *Voice of the Vanishing Minority: Robert Sellar and the* Huntington Gleaner, *1863–1919*. Montreal-Kingston: McGill–Queen's Univ. Press, 1999.

Hilscher, Herb, and Miriam Hilscher. *Alaska, U.S.A.* Boston: Little, Brown, 1959.

Hinckley, Ted C. *The Americanization of Alaska, 1867–1897*. Palo Alto: Pacific Books, 1972.

Hines, John Chesterfield. *Minstrel of the Yukon: An Alaskan Adventure*. New York: Greenburg, 1948.
———. *Wolf Dogs of the North*. Philadelphia: Chilton, 1948.

Hopkins, J. Castell. *Progress of Canada in the Century*. Toronto: Linscott, 1902.

Hrdlicka, Ales. *Alaska Diary, 1926–1931*. Lancaster, PA: The Jaques Cattell Press, 1943.

Hunt, William R. *Alaska: A Bicentennial History*. New York: Norton, 1976.
———. *Arctic Passage: The Turbulent History of the Land and People of the Bering Sea, 1867–1975*. New York: Scribner, 1975.
———. *Distant Justice: Policing the Alaska Frontier*. Norman: Univ. of Oklahoma Press, 1987.
———. *North of 53: The Wild Days of the Alaska–Yukon Mining Frontier*. New York: Macmillan, 1974.

James, William. *The Principles of Psychology*. 1890. Reprint, Cambridge, MA: Harvard Univ. Press, 1983.

Johnson, Paul. *A History of the American People*. San Francisco: HarperPerennial, 1999.

Killen, Linda. *The Russian Bureau: A Case Study in Wilsonian Diplomacy*. Lexington: Univ. of Kentucky Press, 1983.

Kitchener, L. D. *Flag over the North*. Seattle: Superior Publishing, 1954.

Krug, John W., and Caryl Sale Krug. *One Dog Short: The Odyssey and Collection of a Family in Alaska during the Gold Rush*. Juneau: Alaska Department of Education, 1998.

Kunkel, Jeff, ed., *Alaska Gold: Life on the New Frontier, 1898–1906*. San Francisco: Scotwall Associates, 1997.

Kutz, Kenneth J., ed. *Nome Gold: Two Years of the Last Great Gold Rush in American History, 1900–1902*. Darien, CT: Gold Fever Publishing, 1991.

LaFeber, Walter. *The New Empire: An Interpretation of American Expansionism, 1860–1898*. Ithaca: Cornell Univ. Press, 1967.

Lautaret, Ronald, ed. *Alaskan Historical Documents since 1867*. Jefferson, NC: Mcfarland, 1989.

Lockley, Fred. *History of the First Free Delivery System of Mail in Alaska at Nome in 1900*. Seattle: Shorey Book Store, 1966.

Lomen, Carl J. *Fifty Years in Alaska*. New York: David McKay, 1954.

Lomen, Helen. *Taktuk: An Arctic Boy*. Garden City, NY: Doubleday, 1928.

Lucas, Christopher J. *American Higher Education: A History*. New York: St. Martin's Griffin, 1994.

Ludwig, Arnold M. *How Do We Know Who We Are? A Biography of the Self*. Oxford: Oxford Univ. Press, 1997.

MacGowan, Michael. *The Hard Road to Klondike*. London: Routledge and Kegan Paul, 1962.

Madsen, Charles. *Arctic Trader*. New York: Dodd, Mead, 1957.

Martin, Louise Anita. *North to Nome*. Chicago: Albert Whitman, 1939.

Mayhew, Eleanor Ransom, and Ellsworth Luce West. *Captain's Papers*. Barre, MA: Barre Publishing, 1965.

McAdams, Dan P. *The Stories We Live By: Personal Myths and the Making of the Self*. New York: Guilford, 1993.

McClain, Carrie M. *Gold-Rush Nome*. Portland, OR: Graphic Arts Center, 1969.

McDougall, Walter. *Let the Sea Make a Noise: A History of the North Pacific Rim from Magellan to MacArthur*. New York: Basic Books, 1993.

McKee, Lanier. *The Land of Nome*. New York: Grafton, 1902.

Merk, Frederick. *Manifest Destiny and Mission in American History*. Cambridge, MA: Harvard Univ. Press, 1966 (reprint 1995).

Meyer, Karl, and Shareen Brysac. *Tournament of Shadows: The Great Game and the Race for Empire in Asia*. London: Abacus, 1999.

Miller, Orlando. *The Frontier in Alaska and the Matanuska Colony*. New Haven: Yale Univ. Press, 1975.

Mitchell, Donald Craig. *Sold American: The Story of Alaska Natives and Their Land, 1867–1959*. Hanover, NH: Univ. Press of New England, 1997.

Moessner, Victoria Joan, and Joanne E. Gates, eds. *The Alaska–Klondike Diary of Elizabeth Robins, 1900*. Fairbanks: Univ. of Alaska Press, 1999.

Morgan, Lael. *Good Time Girls of the Yukon Gold Rush*. Fairbanks: Epicenter, 1998.

Morse, Kathryn. *The Nature of Gold: An Environmental History of the Klondike Gold Rush*. Seattle: Univ. of Washington Press, 2003.

Nansen, Fridtjof. *Through Siberia: The Land of the Future*. Trans. Arthur G. Chater. New York: Frederick A. Stokes, 1912.

Naske, Claus-M. *Alaska: A History of the 49th State*. Norman: Univ. of Oklahoma Press, 1987.

Naske, Claus-M., and Ludwig J. Rowinski. *Alaska: A Pictorial History*. Virginia Beach: Donning, 1983.

Neering, Rosemary. *Continental Dash: The Russian-American Telegraph*. Gouges, BC: Horsdal and Schubart, 1989.

Nichols, Jean Paddock. *Alaska: A History of its Administration, Exploitation, and Industrial Development during its First Half Century under the Rule of the United States*. Cleveland: Arthur H. Clark, 1924.

Nielson, Jonathan M. *Armed Forces on a Northern Frontier: The Military in Alaska's History, 1867–1987*. New York: Greenwood, 1988.

Niven, Jennifer. *Ada Blackjack: A True Story of Survival in the Arctic*. New York: Hyperion, 2003.

Orth, Donald J. *Dictionary of Alaska Place Names*. Washington, DC: Government Printing Office, 1971.

Owram, Doug. *The Promise of Eden: The Canadian Expansionist Movement and the Idea of the West, 1865–1900*. Toronto: Univ. of Toronto Press, 1992.

Palmer, Lawrence. *Raising Reindeer in Alaska*. Washington, DC: U.S. Department of Agriculture, 1934.

Penlington, Norman. *The Alaska Boundary Dispute: A Critical Reappraisal*. Toronto: McGraw-Hill Ryerson, 1972.

Porsild, Charlene. *Gamblers and Dreamers: Women, Men and Community in the Klondike*. Vancouver: Univ. of British Columbia Press, 1998.

Reed, Irving McKenny. *Boyhood in the Nome Gold Camp*. College, AK: Mineral Industry Research Laboratory, 1969.

Richards, Eva Louis Alvey. *Arctic Mood: A Narrative of Arctic Adventures*. Caldwell, ID: Caxton, 1949.

Rickard, T. A. *Through the Yukon and Alaska*. San Francisco: Mining and Scientific Press, 1909.

Ricker, Elizabeth M. *Seppala: Alaskan Dog Driver*. Boston: Little, Brown, 1930.

Roberts, J. M. *Twentieth Century: The History of the World, 1901–Present*. New York: Penguin, 1999.

Ross, George W., ed. *Patriotic Recitations and Arbor Day Exercises*. Toronto: Warwick Brothers and Rutter, 1893.

Salisbury, Gay, and Laney Salisbury. *The Cruelest Miles: The Heroic Story of Dogs and Men in a Race against an Epidemic*. New York: Norton, 2003.

Samson, Sam. *The Eskimo Princess*. Boston: Christopher Publishing House, 1951.

Savage, Alma Helen. *Smoozie: The Story of an Alaskan Reindeer Fawn*. New York: Sheed and Ward, 1941.

Schiels, Archie. *Seward's Icebox: A Few Notes on the Development of Alaska, 1867–1932.* Bellingham, WA: Union Printing Company, 1933.

Schlereth, Thomas J. *Victorian America: Transformations in Everyday Life, 1876–1915.* New York: HarperPerennial, 1991.

Scully, Julia. *Outside Passage: A Memoir of an Alaskan Childhood.* New York: Random House, 1978.

Sherwood, Morgan B. *Exploration of Alaska, 1865–1900.* New Haven: Yale Univ. Press, 1965.

Shrader, Frank L., and Alfred H. Brooks. *Preliminary Report on the Cape Nome Gold Region.* Washington, DC: Government Printing Office, 1900.

Sears, Stephen W. *Gettysburg.* New York: Houghton Mifflin, 2003.

Simpson, Sherry. *The Way Winter Comes: Alaska Stories.* Seattle: Sasquatch, 1998.

Spence, Clark C. *The Northern Gold Fleet: Twentieth-Century Dredging in Alaska.* Urbana: Univ. of Illinois Press, 1996.

Stacey, John F. *To Alaska for Gold.* 1916. Reprint, Fairfield, WA: Ye Galleon Press, 1973.

Stefansson, Vilhjalmur. *The Adventure of Wrangel Island.* New York: Macmillan, 1925.
———. *Discovery: The Autobiography of Vilhjalmur Stefansson.* New York: McGraw-Hill, 1964.
———. *The Friendly Arctic: The Story of Five Years in Polar Regions.* 1921. Reprint, New York: Greenwood, 1969.
———. *My Life with the Eskimo.* 1913. Reprint, New York: Collier Books, 1966.
———. *The Northward Course of Empire.* New York: Macmillan, 1924.
———. *Northwest to Fortune: The Search of Western Man for a Commercially Practical Route to the Far East.* New York: Duell, Sloan and Pearce, 1958.

Stevenson, Louise L. *The Victorian Homefront: American Thought and Culture, 1860–1900.* Ithaca: Cornell Univ. Press, 1991.

Sundborg, George. *Opportunity in Alaska.* New York: Macmillan, 1945.

Swenson, Olaf. *Northwest of the World: Forty Years of Trading and Hunting in Northern Siberia.* New York: Dodd, Mead, 1944.

Talbot, Winthrop, ed. *Americanization: Principles of Americanism, Essentials of Americanization, Technic of Race-Assimilation.* New York: H. W. Wilson Co., 1917.

Tindall, George Brown, and David Emory Shi. *America: A Narrative History.* New York: Norton, 1999.

Townsend, Leroy Stewart. *The Alaska Gold Rush Letters and Photographs of Leroy S. Townsend, 1898–1899.* Auke Bay, AK: Klondike Research, 1999.

Traxel, David. *1898: The Birth of the American Century.* New York: Vintage, 1998.

Tuttle, Charles R. *Alaska: Its Meaning to the World, Its Resources, Its Opportunities.* Seattle: Franklin Shuey, 1914.

Underwood, John Jasper. *Alaska: An Empire in the Making.* New York: Dodd, Mead, 1912.

Ungermann, Kenneth A. *The Race to Nome: The Story of the Heroic Alaskan Dog Teams that Rushed Diphtheria Serum to Stricken Nome in 1925.* New York: Harper and Row, 1963.

Vanderlip, Washington B., and Homer B. Hulbert. *In Search of a Siberian Klondike.* New York: Century, 1903.

Welzl, Jan. *Thirty Years in the Golden North.* Trans. Paul Selver. New York: Macmillan, 1932.

Wharton, David B. *The Alaska Gold Rush.* Bloomington: Indiana Univ. Press, 1972.

Wheeler, Keith. *The Alaskans*. Alexandria, VA: Time-Life Books, 1977.

Wheeler, William Bruce, and Susan D. Becker, eds. *Discovering the American Past: A Look at the Evidence,* vol. 2. New York: Houghton Mifflin, 1998.

Whiting, Fenton Blakemore. *Grit, Grief and Gold*. Seattle: Peacock, 1933.

Wickersham, James. *Old Yukon: Tails, Trails, and Trials*. Washington, DC: Washington Law Book Co., 1938.

Wightman, F. A. *Our Canadian Heritage, Its Resources and Possibilities*. Toronto: William Briggs, 1905.

Williams, Gerald O. *The Bering Sea Fur Seal Dispute, 1885–1911*. Juneau: Alaska Maritime Publications, 1984.

Willoughby, Barrett. *Alaska Holiday*. Boston: Little, Brown, 1940.
———. *The Trail Eater*. New York: Putnam, 1929.

Wirt, Loyal. *Alaskan Adventures*. New York: 1937.

Woodman, Lyman. *Duty Station Northwest: The U.S. Army in Alaska and Western Canada*. 2 vols. Anchorage: Alaska Historical Society, 1996–1997.

INDEX

Page numbers in *italics* refer to figures.